TRANSFORMING DIALOGUE

The Relational Dimension of The Lord's Prayer

TRANSFORMING DIALOGUE

The Relational Dimension of The Lord's Prayer

CHRISTINE WOOD

WINEPRESS WP PUBLISHING

Printed in the United States of America

Packaged by WinePress Publishing, PO Box 428, Enumclaw, WA 98022.

LIFE DESIGN
PO Box 7295
Ventura, CA 93006-7295

For information regarding the Life Design program and community outreach, please call:
805-658-8088

ISBN 1-57921-180-1
Library of Congress Catalog Card Number: 00-101086

CONTENTS

More things are wrought by prayer than this world dreams of.
Wherefore, let thy voice rise like a fountain, night and day.

— Alfred Lord Tennyson

LESSON ONE

Warm Up for *TRANSFORMING DIALOGUE*

Read Aesop's fable, The Tortoise and the Hare.

Once upon a time there was a hare who, boasting how he could run faster than anyone else, was forever teasing the tortoise for its slowness. Then one day, the irate tortoise answered back: "Who do you think you are? There's no denying you're swift, but even you can be beaten!" The hare squealed with laughter.

"Beaten in a race? By whom? Not you, surely! I bet there's nobody in the world that can win against me, I'm so speedy. Now, why don't you try?"

Annoyed by such bragging, the tortoise accepted the challenge. The next day at dawn they stood at the starting line. The hare yawned sleepily as the meek tortoise trudged slowly off. When the hare saw how painfully slow his rival was, he decided, half asleep on his feet, to have a quick nap. "Take your time!" he said. "I'll have forty winks and catch up with you in a minute."

The hare woke with a start from a fitful sleep and gazed round, looking for the tortoise. But the creature was only a short distance away, having barely covered a third of the course. Breathing a sigh of relief, the hare decided he might as well have breakfast too, and off he went to munch some cabbages he had noticed in a nearby field. But the heavy meal and the hot sun made his eyelids droop. With a careless glance at the tortoise, now halfway along the course, he decided to have another snooze before flashing past the winning post. And, smiling at the thought of the look on the tortoise's face when it saw the hare speed by, he fell asleep and was soon snoring happily. The sun started to sink below the horizon, and the tortoise, who had been plodding towards the winning post since morning, was scarcely a yard from the finish. At that very point, the hare woke with a jolt. He could see the tortoise a speck in the distance and away he dashed. He leapt and bound at a great rate, his tongue lolling, and gasping for breath. Just a little more and he'd be the first at the finish. But the hare's last leap was just too late, for the tortoise had beaten him to the winning post. Poor hare! Tired and in disgrace, he slumped down beside the tortoise who was silently smiling at him.

"Slowly does it every time!" he said.

Select which of these two creatures best describes how you approach learning. *Explain* your choice.

LESSON ONE

PREFACE

Slow me down, God, and inspire me to send my roots deep into the soil of life's enduring values that I may grow toward the stars and unfold my destiny.
—Wilfred Peterson

Read the following information. *Mark* what is useful to you.

We've entered a century marked by seismic changes, creating a different world and a whole new way of dealing with things that were inconceivable only a few years ago. Every day we are presented with something new we need to learn. The fact that a weekday edition of the New York Times holds more information than a citizen living 300 years ago had to process in their entire lifetime reveals the scope of the information we're presented with every day. We often stand numb in the deluge. What information do we need to learn to create a meaningful life in the midst of this sophisticated, constantly changing world?

David Orr makes a distinction between the kinds of knowledge we need to effectively navigate through this new world. "Fast knowledge" is the information we need to keep up with our fast-paced, always changing culture. It's marked by knowledge of technology. For us to live effectively in this new century requires that we are educated in computers, automated services, and sophisticated machines and appliances. But everything that we need to know does not fall beneath the breaking wave of "fast knowledge."

We also need "slow knowledge," an education in the wisdom that will prepare us for life in today's world. "Slow knowledge" is required for us to carefully select only what will benefit us. Our selection will be based on our values and priorities. "Slow knowledge" makes life meaningful while living in a fast-paced world.

In *Transforming Dialogue* you will be learning "slow knowledge" about prayer. If you could look back at the most dynamic Christians throughout the past 20 centuries, you would discover that these men and women are connected by the common belief that prayer was the main business of their lives. To be educated in prayer requires that we be involved in "slow knowledge." This means that we may need to slow down in order to learn how to pray wisely. My own experience with prayer has been that I am a "tortoise" learner and that God never fails to take me as I am and move me slowly to a deeper place. Tortoises have to learn "fast knowledge" to survive and hares need to learn "slow knowledge" and the wisdom gained from it. It is my hope that as you study the teachings of Jesus on prayer, you will discover in a refreshing way that God is on your side as you live in this world which is marked by possibility, uncertainty, and need. He is present and He is not silent. God is inviting you to establish an affirming dialogue with Him in prayer.

The end of learning is
to know God,
and out of that knowledge
to love him
and to imitate him...
—John Milton

Summarize what was useful to you in the above information.

Identify which kind of knowledge you are most comfortable with—"fast" or "slow".

Read the FOCUS to Transforming Dialogue study. *Mark* what is useful to you.

FOCUS

> ***The great thing is prayer. Prayer itself. If you want a life of prayer, the way to get it is by praying . . . . You start where you are and you deepen what you already have.***
> **—Thomas Merton**

Two thousand years ago, Jesus Christ entered human history, creating a tidal wave of change. By any measure, He is the dominant figure in Western civilization.[1] Even today, He continues to transform the lives of people who believe in Him and live by His power. The first disciples of Jesus, those who knew Him best, observed a vital link between the prayers of Jesus, how He lived, and what He was able to do. They watched Jesus live by a habit of prayer. Luke said, "Jesus often withdrew to lonely places and prayed" (Luke 5:16). For this reason, they approached Jesus with this request, "Lord, teach us to pray . . ." (Luke 11:1). The reply Jesus gave is what is referred to as "The Lord's Prayer." It's a prayer often spoken at weddings, funerals, and weekly church services. Perhaps you have read or heard it before:

> Our Father in heaven,
> hallowed be your name,
> your kingdom come,
> your will be done
> on earth as it is in heaven.
> Give us today our daily bread.
> Forgive us our debts,
> as we also have forgiven our debtors.
> And lead us not into temptation,
> but deliver us from the evil one.
> (Matthew 6: 9–13)

It's entirely possible that this prayer is a succinct synopsis of Jesus' teachings to His disciples over a long period of time. While the word "dialogue" does not appear in the prayer, the words convey our interaction is required. Each phrase in the Lord's prayer can easily be customized to

---

[1] For a secular analysis of this, refer to *Newsweek Magazine,* March 29, 1999.

your needs for that day. For example, you can use the phrase "Your will be done" to ask God for His will to be made known to you concerning how to deal with Bill, a difficult customer. You can ask God for His will to be done as you work through a complicated insurance problem. Every need you have constitutes an opportunity to pray. In the lessons ahead we will look at how He communicates His will to us when we are specific in prayer.

Learning how to listen is a skill that grows through practice. Just as listening precedes speaking in children's language development, so listening to God is the first step of prayer. He will give you an awareness of your needs. As you become attuned to His voice, you will pray for these needs, and your prayers will develop depth through an ongoing dialogue with God concerning them.

Peter Senge gives this helpful description about the nature of dialogue.

> There is an old distinction in our culture that it is time to reexamine. It has to do with the words "dialogue" and "discussion." The word "dialogue" comes from the Greek dia-logos. Logos means meaning or word; dia means through. The original meaning of the word "dia-logos" was meaning moves through or flow of meaning. When a group of people talk with one another so that there is a flow of meaning, this is a very special type of conversation. We become unconcerned about who says what, about whose view prevails, or who saves face. We enter the domain of truly thinking together. By contrast, the word "discussion" comes from the same roots as "percussion" and "concussion." It literally means to break apart. A discussion involves heaving one's views at one another. Who wins and who loses is often all that matters. Quite an interesting contrast in images. Meaning moving through versus heaving one's views at the other.

List some qualities a person might need to be able to dialogue. (Example, patience to listen. . .)

Recall your last gathering of family or good friends. *Name* what characterized the conversation. Was it a "dialogue" or a "discussion?"

Continue to *read* the FOCUS, *marking* what strikes you as important.

> *To pray is to change. Prayer is the central avenue God uses to transform us.*
> **—Richard Foster**

The disciples of Jesus asked Him to teach them to pray because they wanted their lives to be transformed; they wanted the relationship with God that Jesus had. In the Lord's Prayer, Jesus showed His disciples if they wanted transformed lives, they would have to use the principles of dialogue. Dialogue between humans takes place among equals. To enter into a dialogue with God, we must acknowledge from the beginning that we are coming to one who is superior to us in every way. Dialogue with God means entering the domain of thinking about our lives together with God in terms of His values and His priorities. We speak to God and we listen to Him. He gives us knowledge of His way to live. The disciples in Jesus' day received this knowledge through being physically present with Jesus. Today, His life becomes real to us through the study of scripture. As our knowledge of Jesus develops, we become aware of the gap between His way of living and our own. This knowledge creates a need in us, and this need informs us about how to pray. Here are some of the needs Jesus addressed in the Lord's Prayer:

- Our need to know and experience God as a loving, heavenly Father who is competent to help us with whatever need we have;
- Our need to know and live by the principles He has established, principles that work for our benefit;
- Our personal daily needs, no matter how small or how great;
- Our need to be forgiven when we have wronged God or somebody else;
- Our need to practice forgiveness toward those who have wronged us;
- Our need to be delivered from unnecessary trials and the presence of evil.

As you study the Lord's prayer, I believe you will find that it is comprehensive enough to include every human need. Our need can come from something as simple as fatigue or as complex as personal failure. Times inevitably come when, regardless of age, gender, the height of our success or depth of our failure, we want or need to call out for help to the One who is competent to help us. Prayer is asking our Heavenly Father for what we need and receiving it. It is God's nature to hear and to answer prayer. Most of us have had some experience with praying. Through studying the model of prayer Jesus taught, we can become more effective in knowing what we actually need and knowing how to ask God to help us. *Transforming Dialogue* study is offered to you in the anticipation that you will develop the slow knowledge to experience a deeper personal relationship with God as you learn to dialogue with Him in prayer.

Identify some things you would like to learn or accomplish during this study.

HOW *TRANSFORMING DIALOGUE* IS DESIGNED

Prior to beginning Lesson Two *read* the following which outlines how the lessons that follow are organized.

During this study, think of yourself as a participant. You will be learning about the Lord's Prayer by studying it and applying what you learn to your own life.

Life Design studies consist of two main segments:

PERSONAL STUDY: This book contains lessons to complete before meeting with your small group;

SMALL GROUP: If you meet in a group to discuss the lesson, you will have an opportunity to learn even more from the insights offered by others.

During the course of each lesson you will learn how to:

- *Slow down* and *listen* to God's inspiring voice;
- *Develop* deep roots in God's enduring values;
- *Pray* for yourself in ways that will bring life into your living;
- *Pray* for others in the same way.

We learn by doing. For this reason lessons will emphasize in *Italics* a task or action to take. Each lesson contains four cooperative parts; each essential for a complete learning experience.

I. Quiet Time for FOCUS

To fully understand and appreciate the lessons, set aside quiet time on your calendar each week for your study. Give study the same priority you would any important appointment. Create a pleasant and quiet place for yourself. Enhance your study space with a comfortable pillow, candle, a cup of coffee, or soft drink—anything that invites you to enjoy learning.

Each Life Design lesson begins with a FOCUS section that introduces the topic and its biblical perspective. If you are new to Bible study, you will find concepts that may, at first, seem foreign. It is vital that the FOCUS material is clear to you and that you identify where you stand in relationship to it. The questions about the FOCUS section help prepare you for the Bible study that follows.

2. Personal Study

In this section, you will discover what the Bible says about the lesson topic. Since Life Design lessons are designed for the whole person, you will investigate and evaluate your thoughts, feelings, and behaviors in light of biblical principles. What you learn in your private study prepares you to participate in the next activity.

3. Follow Through

After studying the topic privately, take time to reflect on your discoveries. You may find it helpful to work on this throughout the week as you see new insights emerge and find ways to integrate what you have learned into your own personal life. You will be amazed at how quickly the Bible "comes alive" when you apply it personally.

4. Group Learning

This section of the lesson is to be done together in your small group. Your group will contain people of every sort who may not be in your usual sphere of friendships. You will be introduced to new ideas and approaches to situations. Here is where someone else's personal point of view and life experience may turn out to be just the insight you need but don't have the resources to create on your own.

LESSON TWO
Up Close and Personal

Prayer is simply children walking
and talking with our Father at hand.
—Dallas Willard

Read the FOCUS. *Mark* what is useful to you.

FOCUS

Luke tells us that one day, after the disciples had watched Jesus pray, one of them said, "Lord, teach *us* to pray." *This is the only record in the New Testament of the disciples asking Jesus to teach them something.* The disciples had lived with Jesus, listened to Him teach, watched Him interact with people, and they had come to a point where they wanted to be just like Him. Here was a man who was joyful in celebration, merciful in the face of every kind of need, and decisive in dealing with challenges and problems. They saw in Jesus the fullness of an up close and personal relationship with God. They had simply never heard of or seen anyone quite like Him. They knew that prayer was the source of His remarkable life.

I understand a little of what motivated them to ask Jesus to teach them how to pray. Soon after becoming a Christian, I became a leader in Bible Study Fellowship, a lay Bible school founded by A. Wetherell Johnson. During my first year of leadership, I attended a leadership conference led by her. When I first heard her pray, I felt as though the invisible curtain had been parted between earth and heaven. I was able to see for the first time in my life how thrilling and satisfying an up close and personal relationship with God in prayer could be. I wanted this same connection. This experience transformed my understanding of God and of prayer. It marked the beginning of my commitment to pray, to press in to know God intimately and to experience His tenderness and the wisdom of His counsel.

In the Old Testament the concept of God as Father was used to describe the covenant relationship between God and Israel (Exodus 4:22, Deuteronomy 32:6). Later, in the Garden of Gethsemane, Jesus called His Father "Abba", which in the Aramaic language of the New Testament is parallel to our use of "daddy" or "papa." This was the most intimate name Jesus could have used with His Father revealing the tender, nurturing and compassionate nature of their relationship.

It must have been shocking for the disciples to hear God addressed as "Father" for two reasons. In the first place, the Jews thought the word "God" was so holy, they never spoke it aloud. This familiar and personal address would have been inconceivable to the disciples until they saw Jesus use it.

In the second place, fathers in the Roman world where the disciples lived had complete authority. They could speak one word, and their son or daughter would be sold into slavery or abandoned. Fathers were feared by their children. Surely the disciples thought of this when they heard Jesus address God as "Father." They had some issues to work through, as do many of us who come from families with less than ideal parents. Coming to God on this basis may not be natural or easy.

O you who answer prayer! To you all flesh shall come.
—Psalm 65:2 NRSV

The instinct to pray is as natural as breathing. We have a basic need for prayer, a basic hope that there is a God who will hear us. Jesus teaches us that the God who is listening is "Abba Father." He is not abstract, hard, or impersonal. He is the ideal father, personal, tender, and compassionate.

If we are to approach prayer as a transforming dialogue in which we come to share our life with God and He shares His life with us, we have to learn to trust God as a loving Father. If we have had problems with our earthly dad, we will probably struggle with this. It will take time. At this moment, just consider that it's important not to throw out the baby with the bath water. Just stick your toe into the bath and ease your way in. Move at a pace that is comfortable for you. As we learn to look to God as a father, we discover that we can be up close and personal and open and honest with him, just as we would be with an ideal father. In turn, He speaks to us and we learn to recognize His voice and trust Him. We discover that God is always speaking to us. He speaks to us through scripture, Christian teaching, books, other people, and in the course of the events of our life, both common and extraordinary.

Our Father in Heaven, hallowed be your name…
—Matthew 6:9

Unless we can relate to God on the basis of trust, we cannot interact with Him to change our lives. Transformation requires trust, which grows through the practice of interactive prayer. Is it any wonder, then, that people who engage in a transforming dialogue with God find ultimate fulfillment in experiencing God as "Abba Father?"

QUIET TIME FOR FOCUS

1. Summarize What Was Useful to You in the FOCUS

Summarize what you marked as important to you in the FOCUS.

2. Look at Your Experience with God as Your Heavenly Father

The following questions require self-reflection. Pausing to look at how you have lived or are living will enable you to see what has been going on in your experience with God and with prayer. If you are unaccustomed to doing this, you are not alone. In our noisy, crowded world, there is little time or encouragement to reflect. If any of these questions seem difficult to answer at first, just leave it. Later, if insight comes to you, fill in the empty spaces. These are personal questions, and if you are meeting in a small group you will not be called on to share your answers.

Complete the following sentences:

When God invites me to be up close and personal with Him, I . . .

Things that help me see God as my loving Father are . . .

The things that challenge my ability to see God as my loving Father are . . .

3. Pray for Guidance with This Lesson

Write a prayer asking God to teach you about being up close and personal with Him.

PERSONAL STUDY

1. The Relational Emphasis of The Lord's Prayer

Read the following aloud, emphasizing the words in italics.

> *Our* Father in heaven, hallowed be your name, your kingdom come, your will be done on earth as it is in heaven. Give *us* this day *our* daily bread. Forgive *us* our debts, as *we* also have forgiven *our* debtors. And lead *us* not into temptation, but deliver *us* from the evil one (Matthew 6:9–13).

a. *List* what strikes you as important when you read the prayer with this emphasis?

b. *State* how this emphasis might influence how you pray for:

- People you enjoy?
- People that upset you?
- People who are in need?
- Yourself?

God doesn't just love you because he has to, he loves you because he wants to. God delights in you. Of course, that doesn't mean God delights in everything you do. Your own mother doesn't do that, if she's at all healthy. But the fact that you exist—you, your own self—is very good in God's eyes. God likes to love you.
—John Ortberg

2. The Father Heart of God

a. *Read* Luke 15:11–32 from the point of view that the father in this story illustrates the qualities of God as Father. *Record* as many characteristics of this father as you can find.

b. *Reread* this parable aloud. *State* how this story reveals the knowledge and love the father had for each of his sons.

Younger Son	Older son

c. *Specify* whether you think the older son saw his father in verses 28–30 as "my father" or "the father my brother and I share." How did this view of his father shape his attitudes and behavior?

3. Pray to Our Father in Heaven

a. In the Bible, when the word "heaven" occurs, it sometimes refers to the high and lofty abode where God dwells. *Describe* what happens in this place.

- Deuteronomy 26:15

- Psalm 57:3

- Psalm 102:19–20

b. *Examine* how being convinced that God is like this might impact how a person prays.

c. The word "heaven" also means the atmospheric space immediately surrounding us. In Matthew 6:9 the word "heaven" literally means air or atmosphere. It is accurate to interpret this as meaning God is present in the unseen realm immediately surrounding us. *Describe* how God is portrayed in the following texts.

- 2 Chronicles 16:9

- 2 Kings 6:16–17 (Here, the prophet Elisha was encouraging his servant who was terrified of a large, enemy army that surrounded the city where they were staying.)

- Acts 17:24–28

d. *Analyze* how trusting that your heavenly Father is as close as your own breath might influence how you pray.

4. "Hallowed" Be Your Name

In Matthew 6:9, Jesus declares God's name is hallowed. Names in the Bible are never "just" names. They always signify something beyond the surface, the facets of a person's stature or character.

a. *Read* Dallas Willard's definition of "hallowed". *Mark* what strikes you as important.

   Very few people any longer understand what it means to "hallow" something and are apt to associate hallow only with ghosts and Halloween. So we would do better to translate the language here as let your name be sanctified. Let it be uniquely respected. Let it be rendered holy. Really, the idea is that his name should be treasured and loved more than any other, held in an absolutely unique position among humanity.

b. *Read* Isaiah 6:1–8. Isaiah was a faithful prophet who lived six centuries before Christ. He lived to see Israel suffer the consequences of failing to "hallow" the name of God. *Describe* Isaiah's vision from God in your own words.

- What did he *see?*

- What did he *hear?*

- What *physical sensations* did he experience?

- What *emotions* did he feel?

c. *Explain* the reason for Isaiah's attitude shift in verse 8.

d. *Name* the ways God communicates with Isaiah. How does Isaiah's experience demonstrate the "dialogue" aspect of prayer?

e. *Describe* how a biblical understanding of God's holiness might influence who and what we pray for.

FOLLOW THROUGH

Read the lesson summary. *Mark* what is useful to you

> ***More than half of our nation's adults pray daily and the amount of time spent on prayer is less than five minutes.***
> **—George Barna**

I. Lesson Summary

The process of developing a relationship with Abba Father[2] is very much like the human process of learning to trust our parents. We come into life helpless and we first make our needs known by crying. When our parents meet those needs, trust begins to be established. That fundamental base for trust is how we learn to function in other relationships, including our relationship with God. Our human experiences influence our spiritual development.

If one or both of our parents prove untrustworthy, we will likely have a difficult time trusting other people; we will have a hard time trusting God.

Fortunately, we can change. We can learn to trust God who wants to help us through any difficulties we may have of drawing near to Him. For some of us this may take a great deal of time. God understands. He is patient with us in our process. God has a "holy" purpose for our lives. Behind all the challenges and pain we face, He extends an invitation to "keep His commands and follow His ways". As we bring our lives in line with His, just as the foolish young son did, we learn how to be up close and personal with God. We begin to understand that whoever we are, whatever we have done or not done, God is with us and He loves us. He stands beside us as a tender and holy heavenly Father, with His arms outstretched in welcome.

---

[2] For information on how to begin a relationship with Abba Father, refer to the Appendix.

2. Identify How You Perceive Your Earthly Father and Your Heavenly Father

Read the following list taken from the implied and stated names of God in Psalm 103:1–18. The opposite characteristic is listed in the right column.[3]

Characteristics of God	Opposite Characteristics
Holy	Profane
Forgiving	Holds grudges
Heals	Creates conflict
Brings good out of bad	Harshly critical
Abounding in love	Stingy and aloof
Compassionate	Distant and uninvolved
Renewing	Depleting
Fair	Unfair
Open and honest	Secretive
Gracious	Rude
Patient	Perfectionist
Merciful	Mean
Watching to applaud	Waiting to pounce
Capable and competent	Incapable, incompetent
Sensitive	Indifferent
Self-controlled	Out of control
Rich/many resources	Poor/no resources

Place a √ on the continuum line describing your experience with your earthly father. If your father was always rude you might mark:

Gracious __________________________________√ Rude

Now *put* a X on the spot describing your experience with your heavenly Father like this:

Gracious __________X_______________________√ Rude

What do you discover? *Write* an honest prayer to God about what you are thinking and feeling now, what you need, and what you are willing to do. Use the ADDITIONAL THOUGHTS page.

[3] This exercise is adapted from a similar one in Myra Boone's workbook, *Touching the Hem of His Garment* referenced in the bibliography.

GROUP LEARNING

Read Linda's story. *Form* groups of four to work through the questions that follow.

Linda became a Christian in college. She holds resentment toward her father for not following through on giving her the money he promised for her college expenses. Her parents are divorced, and her father always seems to be struggling financially. He lives in another area and tries to keep in contact with Linda, but she doesn't make it easy for him. Although she is angry with him, she isn't willing to talk to him about it. Linda realizes she needs to pray about her relationship with her father, but she has a difficult time actually doing it.

a. What might God be trying to communicate to Linda through these circumstances?

b. What could Linda do that would help her differentiate between the characteristics of God and the characteristics of her earthly father?

c. How could the phrases, "Our Father" and "hallowed be Thy name" inform Linda about how to use these phrases to pray for herself in this situation?

d. How could Linda pray for her father?

Additional Thoughts

LESSON THREE
Praying with the Biggest Dog

Before we can pray, "Lord, thy kingdom come,"
We must be willing to pray, "My kingdom go."
—Alan Redpath

Read the FOCUS. *Mark* what strikes you as important.

FOCUS

On an ordinary day, and in an unlikely situation, I learned the "big dog" lesson. I was lifting weights at the gym, thinking about a challenging leadership problem I was trying to solve. Suddenly a woman walked by with a tee shirt that said in big letters:

"IF YOU CAN'T RUN WITH THE BIG DOGS, STAY ON THE PORCH!"

That put my problem more into the realm of "privilege" and my job of solving it into perspective. It also gave me a new slant on prayer.

Prayers that accomplish something have certain guidelines in common. I like to think of them as the "big dogs" of prayer. The first request is the biggest dog of all because it requires that we place our will under the leadership of God. After Jesus taught His disciples to approach God as Father, he taught them to pray, "Your kingdom come, Your will be done on earth as it is in heaven". The Kingdom of God is a concept as alien to most of us today as computer science is to an Indian in the Amazon jungle, whose only method of communicating long distances is drums! We have been taught to be self-sufficient and self-reliant, yet if we want to receive answers to our prayers, then we must learn to ask for things according to the principles and priorities of God's kingdom.[4]

Why on earth should we do this? Because it is the most reasonable and meaningful course we can ever take. Other kingdoms come and go but God's kingdom is everlasting (Psalm 145:13). It is the sphere in which God rules and what He wants to happen actually happens.

When we learn to pray for God's kingdom to be accomplished on earth, we pray about the places where we live our lives—our home, our workplace, our school, our neighborhood, our extended family, our gym—every place we spend time. When we ask God for His kingdom to come into these areas, we are saying that we want to live as He would live in these places. We are asking for God to transform us and the places we live by His presence and the principles of His Kingdom.

On the one hand, God's kingdom lives inside us as we surrender our will to His in each area of our lives. On the other hand, God's kingdom permeates the world as we live His life in it. One of the greatest examples of this in the 20th century was Mother Teresa. Think of how God used her to transform the streets of Calcutta because she prayed for God's kingdom to come there and His will to be done there, and then lived out her prayer.

For most of us, bringing God's kingdom to earth has a less dramatic impact than Mother Teresa's, although I'm certain she had no idea when she began to care for the dying poor that her efforts would lead to the Nobel Peace Prize. It might be helpful in this to rethink The Tortoise and the Hare fable. If we want God's kingdom to come to our part of the earth, we need to think of taking one step at a time. We can pray before we rent our next video. "Lord, help me choose a video tonight

---

[4] For information about how to enter God's kingdom refer to the Appendix.

with values consistent with Yours." We can pray about the problems in the office before we go to work. "Lord, help me treat Jim today as You would. Show me what I can do to bring Your peace into our office."

... your kingdom come, your will be done on earth as it is in heaven.
—Matthew 6:10

As we submit to God's rule in our lives, we function in His kingdom while we live in this world. It is a challenging life-style, but we are not alone. God is with us and for us. He is inviting us to engage in a dialogue with Him about the places where we spend time. He has also given His Spirit to teach us what to do and to empower us to do it. As we study the Bible with an open mind and heart, we learn to understand what God wants from us. He speaks to us. We listen and we respond. By experience we learn to recognize God's voice.

When Jesus said, "I have come that they may have life, and have it to the full" (John 10:10), He was referring to the rich and rewarding life God has in store for us. The first rule for tapping into that life is to put our kingdom inside His. We have to look to Him to fulfill our hopes for a meaningful life. God simply did not intend for us to live independently from Him. The biggest dog of prayer helps us step into this relationship with God.

QUIET TIME FOR FOCUS

1. Summarize What Was Useful to You in the FOCUS

Summarize what you marked as important to you in the FOCUS.

2. Prepare for the Study of God's Kingdom

a. *State* some messages you received growing up about being independent and self-sufficient.

b. *Compare* those messages with what the FOCUS states about praying for God's kingdom to come and His will to be done in your life. What do you discover?

c. *List* the things you do that fill your time each week. *Mark* the areas where you have consciously prayed "Your kingdom come, Your will be done."

d. *Examine* the challenges you face as you practice praying for God's will to come into these areas.

3. Pray for Guidance with This Lesson

Identify what you would like God to do for you as you study this lesson.

PERSONAL STUDY

1. Introduction to God's Kingdom

a. *Read* Psalm 145. *List* the characteristics of God and His kingdom that are stated or implied in this Psalm. *Mark* three that you find most appealing or compelling.

b. *Compare* Mark 1:15 and Luke 17:20–21 with the last lesson's statements about God's presence near to us. *Explain* what you think Jesus was teaching about His kingdom.

c. *Imagine* that one of the characteristics of God's kingdom you marked in Psalm 145 were fully present in your life. *Describe* how that might impact your "To Do" list for today.

2. Our Need to Build a Kingdom

Read the following information. *Mark* what is useful to you.

God has placed in our lives certain things over which we have authority. Certainly our young children fall into that category. If we have a supervisory or leadership position at work, our job gives us authority. Our attitudes are certainly dependent on the choices we make, and belong solely to us, as do our beliefs and emotions. Our kingdom also includes our gifts and talents, and even our weak areas where there is potential for growth or change. We have a God-given desire to exercise authority in these areas. Who does not want to overcome a weakness or develop a talent? Dallas Willard describes the scope of our personal "kingdom" like this, "Our 'kingdom' is simply the range of our effective will. Whatever we genuinely have the say over is in our kingdom. And our having the say over something is precisely what places it within our kingdom. In creating human beings God made them to rule, to reign, to have dominion in a limited sphere. Only so can they be persons."

a. *Read* Genesis 1:27–28. *Identify* where our need to have a say over things originated.

b. Verse 28 says we are to subdue the earth. To "subdue" means to bring creation into submission; to acquire knowledge and mastery over something. In scripture conflict is often involved in subduing things. *Name* some things in your sphere of influence over which you have some authority. *Use* the following categories:

- Roles that involve a lot of your time and energy (For example: Being a wife requires my time and energy every day.)

- Work for which you are responsible

- Natural talents and gifts

3. God's Desires Concerning His Kingdom and Ours

a. *Read* Matthew 6:10. *Explain* what you think each phrase means.

- "Your kingdom come"

- "Your will be done"

- "On earth as it is in heaven"

b. *Describe* how this verse might be applied in exercising your authority over a situation where your mechanic failed to repair your brakes properly.

4. Bring God's Will Down to Earth

Read the following verses. *Name* the attitudes and behaviors that characterize citizens in God's kingdom.

- Matthew 18:1–4

- Romans 14:17

- 1 Corinthians 6:9–11[5]

5. The Conflict Between God's Will and Ours

a. *Read* the following information. *Mark* what is useful to you.

It would be much easier to pray for God's will to be done if that's what we really wanted. In reality, we are often inclined to resist God's will. Don't you find it easier to "speak your mind" to a rude person, rather than be considerate? Isn't it often more tempting to want what you don't have rather than be joyful in what you already own? The Bible teaches that when our first parents Adam and Eve sinned, something went awry in their spiritual genetic code and all of us have inherited it. Sin is like a drop of ink that stains all the water in the glass.[6] If we are to pray for God's will to be done, we have to also recognize where and how we are resisting it. The actual doing of God's will takes place as the Holy Spirit supplies us with whatever resources we need to carry it out.

---

[5] "Justify" is *the act, process or state of being declared right with God.* "Sanctify" is *to cleanse or set apart for sacred use; to declare or make holy.*

[6] For a definition of sin refer to the Appendix.

b. *Read* Galatians 5:16–25. *Answer* the following questions.

- Why is there a conflict between "life in the Spirit" and "life in the sinful nature"?

- What happens when a person chooses life in the sinful nature?

- What do you think it means to "keep in step with the Spirit"?

- Suppose a critical or judgmental person tried to keep in step with the Spirit every day for a year. What overall difference do you think it would make in that person's life?

- How do you respond to the possibility of keeping in step with the Spirit over a long period of time?

FOLLOW THROUGH

The purpose of all prayer is to find God's will and make that will our prayer.
—Catherine Marshall

Read the following summary. *Mark* what is useful to you.

It is easy and natural to build our kingdom without giving any consideration to God. Unfortunately, the world has skillfully conditioned us to believe that we are, as William Cullen Bryant so eloquently proposed, "the master of our fate, the captain of our soul."

Gerald May more recently described our lives without any consideration of integrating God's kingdom into our own. "*We carry our destinies on our own shoulders . . . we carve our marks upon the world with our own muscles . . . we must forge some semblance of meaning and purpose through the efforts of our personal willpower. We have been taught very well that meaning and purpose can be achieved only through the exercise of personal mastery and self-determination.*"

While we live in the midst of our own kingdoms, we also live under the influence and pressures of the kingdoms of this world. In the political kingdoms of the world, authority comes from military power. In the glittering kingdom of Hollywood, authority comes from a beautiful image. In the powerful kingdom of finance, authority comes from money. In the prestigious kingdom of education, authority comes from academic degrees. We live under the influence of these kingdoms, even though we often aren't aware of it. More often than not we succumb to their influence and build our own individual kingdoms under their authority.

The most meaningful dimension of life begins when we discover our heavenly Father's kingdom and His intention for our place in it. Once we discover this, we simply place our hand in our Father's and fully function in that space. In His loving and powerful presence, we discover the joy that comes when we engage in a dialogue about how we can bring about His kingdom in that space. Saying "yes" to God, praying with the biggest dog, is a crucial element in prayer. The more costly the consent, the more difficult is the giving of it. Saying "yes" in deeply felt issues requires being able to dialogue with God concerning all the issues involved. Praying this way means that at some point we must actually agree with Him to do His will.

a. *Review* the list you made in Activity 2.b. in the PERSONAL STUDY section of this lesson. *Choose* one that is important to you now.

b. *Select* one of the qualities of "kingdom living" from Activity 4 in the PERSONAL STUDY section of this lesson. *Imagine* how focusing on and applying that quality in the situation you have chosen would change how you think, feel, and behave in that situation.

c. *Describe* how you might feel as a result of staying in step with the Spirit for the next year in that situation.

d. *Write* or *speak* a prayer, asking for God's guidance and strength to bring His kingdom and His will into this area of your life. *Share* your intent with a supportive friend.

GROUP LEARNING

Read the following story. *Form* groups of four to work on the activities that follow.

> Carrie's elderly mother, Betty, lives with her and is difficult to deal with. Betty is strong-willed, and as she ages she is becoming domineering and aggressive about getting her own way. Carrie has a demanding job, and dreads coming home to this every night. She admits to taking the path of least resistance and she has become as cantankerous as her mother. She knows that if she prays for God's kingdom to come to this situation and for His will to be done in her home as it is done in heaven, she's going to have to change. She knows it will take time to sort out this problem and that it's not completely solvable. She wants to pray for this, but she's afraid to face what God's will for her might be.

a. *State* how God is speaking to Carrie in this situation.

b. *Identify* Carrie's places of dominion and *state* the conflict of wills she is dealing with.

c. *Examine* how Carrie might address her fears about facing God's will.

d. *Propose* how Carrie can pray in this situation for herself and for her mother.

Additional Thoughts

LESSON FOUR
The Problem of a Picnic in Pompeii

There is no virtue like necessity.
—Shakespeare

Read the FOCUS. *Mark* what is useful to you.

FOCUS

Imagine that you are a citizen of Pompeii, Italy in 79 A.D. You are living in a beautiful, sophisticated city where signs of affluence are posted everywhere. Beautiful frescos decorate homes and public buildings, food and wine are so plentiful that even slaves are well fed. The huge, bustling market place is crowded with people, including foreign merchants who have sailed into the Port of Pompeii. Before you stretches the Mediterranean Sea. Standing majestically at your back is Mount Vesuvius, quiet for so long it's assumed inactive.

The 21st century affluent Western world has a lot in common with Pompeii in 79 A.D. Today we are caught up with desires often created by the hype that accompanies affluence. For many, the need is not for daily bread, but for a breadmaker with a dozen settings. Needs are often determined by impulse, not necessity. On the fateful day when Mount Vesuvius erupted, no one in Pompeii had any awareness of an immediate, urgent need to flee the city. Totally oblivious of danger until the lava flowed fast and furious through the city, thousands perished. The needs and desires they woke up with that day were inconsequential compared to the overwhelming need to escape Pompeii. Excavations reveal that the volcano erupted so suddenly and violently that at one moment women were baking bread, and the next they were smothered in molten lava.

Asking for will power to avoid tempting trays of delicious breads in the buffet line is not what Jesus meant when he taught us to pray for our daily bread. The needs Jesus referred to were *unavoidable necessities.* These include all the needs that accompany the stresses of modern life with its technological glitches, fast pace, and sophisticated options. We can ask Him to supply our needs, and as we receive God's reply, we will be motivated to move deeper into His kingdom. This is what the disciples also did. They left their work behind and followed Jesus, trusting God for their daily needs, just as Jesus did. This dependency deepened their relationship with God so they continued to work full time for God, even after Jesus was no longer physically with them.

For us, the challenge is to know the difference between what we actually need and what we want. All these things we can bring to God in prayer and learn to hear what He says to us about them. God wants to give us what we need and when we take delight in Him, He will also give us our heart's desires (Psalm 37:4).

Because we are multifaceted people every day brings different physical, mental, spiritual, emotional, and social needs. Our heavenly Father urges us to bring whatever needs we have to Him in prayer. Consider this amazing promise in Philippians 4:6–7. "Do not be anxious about anything, but in everything, by prayer and petition, with thanksgiving, present your requests to God. And the peace of God, which transcends all understanding, will guard your hearts and your minds in Christ Jesus."

Forgive us our debts, as we also have forgiven our debtors.
—Matthew 6:12

Scripture makes it clear that we also need forgiveness every day for the sins we commit against God and each other. To keep short, daily accounts with God, there should be a time in our prayer when we are quiet and ask

God to reveal any wrong we have done to Him, others, and ourselves. We also have a need each day to forgive those who have wronged us.

God's personal provision is not meant to occur within a vacuum. Even as we privately pray, we are still members of a community. Others surround us with their pressing daily needs. No wonder then, that Jesus asks us to pray for *our* daily bread, *our* need for forgiveness, *our* need to be forgiving. As we pray for ourselves and others, our attitudes and affections are daily transformed by our heavenly Father.

Try to imagine what our prayer experience would be like if he (Jesus) had forbidden us to ask for the little things. What if the only things we were allowed to talk about were the weighty matters, the important things, the profound issues? We would be orphaned in the cosmos, cold and terribly alone. But the opposite is true: he welcomes us with our 1,000 trifles for they are each important to him.
—Richard Foster

We have been learning that prayer is asking God for what we need within the framework of dialogue. When we first know God, we tend to tell God what we think we need. This is perfectly fine, but as we grow spiritually we desire to live more fully for God and to impact our world for His kingdom. We begin learning how to pray for the details, the routine events of our daily experience in light of His kingdom. As we verbalize our needs, we learn to analyze them as we listen to God speak to us through His Word, through our ordinary thoughts, through others, and sometimes through vivid images and impressions.

This holy exchange triggers subtle yet profound changes in us. We begin to form different priorities and perspectives. Occasionally we discover that what we wanted is actually unnecessary, undesirable, greedy, or even harmful to ourselves and others. We discover that we were like the self-occupied citizens of doomed Pompeii setting out for a picnic when we should abandon the city. At other times, we happily discover that what we actually want is consistent with our needs and is a gift from our Abba Father. As God answers our prayers, we experience the great joy and pleasure of being a child in His kingdom.

QUIET TIME FOR FOCUS

1. Summarize What Was Useful to You in the FOCUS

Summarize what was useful to you in the FOCUS.

2. Identify the Needs of a Fully Functioning Child in God's Kingdom

Answer the following questions.

a. How do you *differentiate* between your *wants* and your *needs?*

b. *Name* a Christian you know fairly well. What do you think that person needs in order to be a fully functioning person in God's kingdom:

- Physically?
- Mentally?
- Emotionally?
- Socially?
- Spiritually?

c. *Write* a prayer expressing your need for God's guidance in this lesson.

PERSONAL STUDY

1. Pray for What We Need

Read Matthew 6:11. *Answer* the following questions:

a. For what does Jesus teach us to pray?

b. What dimension is added by the words "us" and "our"?

c. *Name* one thing you need every day to function in God's kingdom.

Today even many Christians read and say, "forgive us our trespasses" as "give me a break." In the typically late-twentieth-century manner, this saves the ego and its egotism. "I am not a sinner, I just need a break!" But no, I need more than a break. I need pity because of who I am. If my pride is untouched when I pray for forgiveness, I have not prayed for forgiveness. I don't even understand it.
—Dallas Willard

d. How do you think praying every day this week for that need might influence your experience with God in prayer?

2. Our Greatest Daily Need

a. Jesus teaches about daily needs. *Read* Matthew 6:25–34. *State* what Jesus teaches.

b. *Underline* the word "worry" in this text. *Identify* what people worry about. *Contrast* this with what you tend to worry about. What do you discover?

c. *Examine* verse 33. *Explain* what Jesus says we need the most.

d. *Place* your name at the beginning of verse 33. *Read* it aloud. *Interpret* what it means to you.

e. *Determine* what poses the greatest challenge to you in trusting God to meet your needs to be a citizen in His kingdom.

To belong to God's kingdom means losing a legion of anxieties: what clothes to wear, what we do with our outer appearance to make us more attractive, even what height we try to give ourselves! Instead, prayer helps us to keep our whole lives in proportion. Prayer is more realistic, not less, than our anxieties.
—James Houston

3. Our Daily Need for Forgiveness

a. *Read* Matthew 6:12. The word translated here as "debt" means ***something owed to God because of sins either of commission (action) or omission (ignorance or neglect).*** *Explain* what Jesus is teaching here.

God loves to forgive. It is the one thing He yearns to do, aches to do, rushes to do. At the very heart of the universe is God's desire to give and forgive.
—Richard Foster

b. *Examine* why we need God's help to experience forgiveness and extend it to others.

4. Common Sins

Read Proverbs 6:16–19.

a. *List* the things God hates. *State* where you see these sins *actively* and *passively* committed today.[7]

Sins that God hates:	Where they are committed today:

b. *Identify* what it would take for a person to be able to confess these sins to God and stop the behavior.

c. *Select* one that represents a problem for you. *Describe* its impact on you and those you love.

d. *Explain* why God hates these things.

5. Jesus Teaches About Forgiveness

a. *Read* Matthew 18:21–35. In this parable, *consider* that the king represents God, the slaves represent sinful people. *Identify* what Peter meant by his question in verse 21.

b. *Interpret* Jesus' response in verse 22.

[7] For information on God's remedy for sin, refer to the Appendix.

c. *Describe* what the king did for the slave who owed him 10,000 talents. (A talent was worth more than fifteen years' wages for a laborer.) *Tell* how the king demonstrates the forgiveness of which Jesus spoke.

d. *Explain* why you think the unmerciful servant did not forgive his fellow servant.

e. *Examine* how this parable illustrates the teaching of Matthew 6:12.

FOLLOW THROUGH

People want to know God. They want less to know about God or know about religion than to know God.
—Leonard Sweet

I. Summary

Read the following summary. *Mark* what strikes you as important.

We are living in a time of unparalleled spiritual hunger, yet how often we slip into a "picnic in Pompeii" attitude about the things that are really important. How many needs go unmet because we have either not thought to ask for God's help, or because we thought the need was too small or insignificant in the large scheme of things to "bother" God with? If we are to fully function as a child in God's Kingdom, we daily must bring our needs to God, who has the resources to meet them. We are not alone in a meaningless universe. Our heavenly Father is beside us and He wants to become more real to us through answering our prayers about the things we need.

We must also be careful not to slip into the kind of praying that reveals that we consider our needs or wants greater than the genuine needs of others. The following prayer reflects the folly of doing this:

> *We who seek to maintain a shaky civilization do pray most earnestly that the countries which suffer exploitation may not be angry with the exploiters, that the hungry may not harbor resentment against those who have food, that the down-trodden may take it patiently, that nations with empty larders may prefer starvation to communism, that the "have not" countries may rejoice in the prosperity of those that have, and that all people who have been deeply insulted and despised may have short memories. You can do all things, O God.*
> —David Head

It is easy to laugh at this egocentric prayer, but we dare not laugh long. Instead of being accountable to God and to fellow citizens of the world, this prayer tends to reverse the standard set by Abba Father.

When we do this, we grow deaf to our real needs and insensitive to the sins that fuel our selfish prayers. Dame Julian of Norwich referred to sin as "a lump," that is, we are all in it together. We cannot separate ourselves or anyone else from it. Because of this, we can joyously receive the wisdom of Jesus in teaching us to pray for our daily bread, our sins, and our forgiveness of those who have sinned against us. Only by seeing ourselves through a lens shaded by imperfection, can we see ourselves and others honestly. This opens the door to valid self-acceptance, eventual acceptance of others, and true freedom to live fully as God intended.

2. Function Fully Within God's Kingdom

a. *Identify* the following needs you or a person you love will be facing in the next 24 hours. Be specific.

- Spiritual

- Mental

- Emotional

- Social

- Physical

b. *Pray* frequently for 24 hours for God to meet each of these needs. *Describe* your experience with prayer.

c. *Evaluate* what you learned from this time of prayer that you want to continue to do.

GROUP LEARNING

Form groups of four. *Select* one of the scenarios to work on.

a. You are 20 minutes late for an important meeting. You cannot find a spot in the parking lot. You notice four other cars also looking for spots. You decide to pray for a parking place.

b. You are sitting down to a fabulous family feast after having heard on the news that famine has taken many lives in an African country. You have been asked to thank God for the food on your table.

c. You're sitting in church, about to take communion and you notice Jim seated four rows in front of you. Recently, Jim was rude to you in a committee meeting and you are angry with him. You decide you need to pray about the situation before you take communion.

Imagine that you are the person in the scenario. How would you pray?

Determine how a prayer like that would influence your attitude toward others in that situation.

Share some situations in your life that are similar to the one in your scenario.

Identify ways you can use what you have learned in this lesson to pray for yourself and others in these situations.

ADDITIONAL THOUGHTS

LESSON FIVE
The Truth Behind Virtual Reality

Read the FOCUS. *Mark* what you find most useful.

FOCUS

Technology has opened us up to the world of virtual reality where our senses can be manipulated into believing we are having a *real* experience when, in fact, we are not. We are all impacted by more subtle and pervasive forms of virtual reality through secularization. *Secularism is the way in which whole areas of life, thought, and activity have gradually become independent from biblical authority and the influence of the Church.* Secular influence has virtually taught us to identify reality as what our senses can experience and what our minds can comprehend. But God's truth behind this "reality" is infinitely more.

Assaulted by rush hour traffic, cold winds, a hungry stomach, and a tired body, I stopped to get gas at one of the busiest freeway interchanges in Los Angeles. Everyone was in a hurry; I was also caught up in this hectic scene.The woman ahead of me rushed into the station to buy a pack of cigarettes. Her four year old daughter was honking the horn. The attendant couldn't find her brand of cigarettes. She was very upset, and when her daughter honked the horn for the umpteenth time, she muttered, "If she does that again, I'm going to kill her."

Inwardly I was criticizing this woman when God spoke to me, suggesting I extend His comfort to her. When I put my hand on her arm, she abruptly faced me. "Do you need me to pray for you right now?" I asked. Large tears poured from her eyes as she answered. "Yes. Please pray for my father. He's very ill and I think he's dying. My husband died when our daughter was four months old, my mother died not long after, and now my father. . . Everyone I love has left me." As I prayed for her, I felt God's peace descend on that grimy little building and for the moment I experienced life as sweet and delightful. Beneath the "virtual reality" of this situation, God's "reality" placed me in that gas station to provide gentle support to a pain-soaked woman.

If we compare our life with God's, we discover that we are inherently weaker and cannot stand up against *spiritual* pressure. There is never a moment when we don't *need* strength from God available through His Holy Spirit. The "temptation" Jesus refers to is *anything* that can divert us from, or appear more appealing than God's kingdom and His will (Matthew 6:13). The word for temptation means *to put someone to the test*. The challenges that come into our lives are opportunities to bring God's kingdom down to earth. Yet with each one, we will be tempted to take a lesser path than God's.

Temptations are a form of virtual reality. They appear to be more alluring than God's actual plan. If we could dissect temptations that lead us away from God, we would discover they are as varied as our personalities and circumstances. We are tempted not to "believe" that God loves us or anyone else. We are tempted to "feel" that His kingdom is too restrictive when His will interferes with our own. We are tempted to commit a sin because at the moment, it seems the "best" thing to do. Because the pressures in life can be so stressful and we have poor resistance to temptation, it is wise to pray each day that God would protect us from *unnecessary* trials, and that He will give us strength for those we must bear. Temptations, some so subtle as to be almost unrecognizable at first, set an important task before us: to trust God and renounce whatever pulls us away from being near to Him.

Jesus does not stop with temptation but goes on to pray, "Rescue us from the evil one." Biblical scholarship reveals that Jesus was referring here to

Satan as a living and powerful influence.[8] At its core, the word "evil" means *all things opposed to God.* In teaching us to pray, Jesus boldly confronts the reality of Satan. He is the head of a kingdom opposed to God's. He uses his power and persuasion to tempt us through his "virtual reality" to wander away from God. Jesus gives us a strategy for survival in the face of this evil, so that we can live without fear. Acknowledging evil is such a repugnant thought that many refuse to consider it. This is as dangerous as standing in an open field during a drenching storm, denying the power of lightning because you hear no thunder—best not be holding an open umbrella!

The petition "Lead us not into temptation" really does show us that life is dangerous, that it is something that can trip us up and ruin us, a place where we can stake everything on the wrong card."
—Helmut Thielicke

Evil, though usually unseen, is an undeniable reality. Consider this excerpt from a sermon given by the German theologian, Helmet Thielicke during the Holocaust.

> *Dear friends, in our time we have had far too much contact with demonic powers; we have sensed and seen how men and whole movements have been corrupted and controlled by mysterious, abysmal powers, leading them where they had no intention of going; we have observed all too often how an alien spirit can ride people and change the very substance of men who before may have been quite decent and reasonable persons, driving them to brutalities, delusions of power, and fits of madness which they never appeared to be capable of before; year by year we have seen an increasingly poisonous atmosphere settle down upon our globe and we sense how real and almost tangible are the evil spirits in the air, seeing an invisible hand passing an invisible cup of poison from nation to nation and throwing them into confusion.*

Jesus teaches us to pray for God's rescue from the influence of temptation and evil.

---

[8] The Bible refers to Satan in the following terms: accuser, devil, tempter, evil one, dragon, Beelzebub, Belial, murderer, father of lies, ruler of this world, god of this age, leader of the kingdom of evil, angel of the Abyss, Abaddon, Apollyon, and the ancient serpent.

QUIET TIME FOR FOCUS

1. Summarize What Was Useful to You in the FOCUS

Summarize what you marked as important in the FOCUS.

2. Your Understanding of Temptation and Evil

a. *Name* some things that you are tempted to "think", "feel" or "do" that have the power to draw you away from God's kingdom.

b. *State* what you currently believe about Satan and how you arrived at those beliefs.

c. Suppose the development of Christ-like character required no testing, no trials or effort. *Describe* the kind of Christians this would produce.

d. *Analyze* how viewing temptations as an invitation to draw near to God might influence your response to them.

3. Pray for Your Study of This Lesson

Write a prayer to God about what you need Him to teach you in this lesson dealing with temptation and Satan.

PERSONAL STUDY

Many of the world's most attractive temptations are like some television commercials: frequently deceptive and frightfully costly.
—William Arthur Ward

I. Pray to Overcome Temptation

a. *Read* Matthew 6:13. *Explain* why you think Jesus includes this in His model of what to regularly pray for.

b. *Read* the following list of common temptations. *Distinguish* the most common temptations by *marking* them with an "X". *Mark* the ones most common to you with a *.

____ Participating in habits that dull my appetite for God
____ Neglecting to pray
____ Blaming someone else instead of taking personal responsibility
____ Gossip
____ Refusing to accept the love of Abba Father for me
____ Holding onto resentments
____ Controlling others instead of trusting God to act in their lives
____ Failing to maintain an attitude of gratitude
____ Judging those who are different from me
____ Taking care of personal business on company time
____ Using, rather than cherishing, friends
____ Avoiding confrontation when needed

c. *Notice* again in v. 13 the plural pronouns *us*. *Explain* how knowing other Christians struggle with temptation impacts how you think and feel about them.

2. God's Purpose in Testing Us

a. *Read* the verses below. *Identify* God's purpose in testing us. *Mark* the ones that are especially useful to you.

- Deuteronomy 8:1–5
- Deuteronomy 13:1–4
- Psalm 66:10–12
- I Corinthians 10:6
- James 1:2–4
- I Peter 1:6–7

b. *Read* I Corinthians 10:12–13. *Answer* the following questions.

How are we to view temptation?

What kind of God stands behind our temptations?

What hope is given in this scripture for successfully dealing with temptation?

3. Pray About Evil

Read Matthew 6:13b and Luke 22:31–32.

a. *State* how we can pray concerning evil?

b. *Explain* why prayer is essential in resisting the power of Satan.

4. How Evil Works in Our World

Read the following verses. *Describe* Satan's activities. *Look* for both explicit (directly stated) and implicit (indirectly stated) teaching.

- Matthew 13:19 (Ex: Satan discounts God's word to us.)
- Matthew 16:21–23
- Luke 13:11–16
- John 8:44
- Acts 10:38
- 2 Corinthians 4:3–4
- Revelation 2:9–10

5. The Dual Nature of Satan

a. *Read* the following verses. *State* how Satan is described. *Explain* what you think this means.

- II Corinthians 11:3–4, 13–15

The adversary (Satan) appears as more than a tester of people. He has a quarrel with God, and it is not a lover's quarrel. His question is a sniper's bullet, intended to undermine and destroy. His strategy is to blend truth with falsehood by insinuation and innuendo.
—Gerhard Emanuel Frost

- I Peter 5:8

b. *Compare* these two "personalities" of Satan. What do you discover?

c. *Analyze* how or when you are most often tempted. Which of Satan's dual personalities seems to be most effective in tempting you?

LESSON FIVE

FOLLOW THROUGH

I. SUMMARY

Read the Summary. *Mark* what strikes you as important.

The West appears to have said its definitive farewell to a Christian culture. . . . Our secular colleagues. . . . recognize the debt our civilization owes to the Christian faith to the extent that the faith, having been absorbed by culture itself, has become simply another cultural artifact. Christianity has become a historical factor subservient to a secular culture rather than functioning as the creative power it once was.
—Louis Dupré, Yale Professor

It's taken five centuries for Christianity to reach this state. Behind every step in this long decline, there stood temptations to slip away from the kingdom of God and join with the secular kingdoms that rely on human wisdom and strength. The virtual reality of secularism simply has not brought us to a "better" or even more "enlightened" place.

It is challenging to live in the kingdom of God while living in this world. It's not uncommon for me to talk with fellow Christians who have adopted a secular view on certain issues without even knowing (and sometimes not caring) that they have. If we don't know or don't care about what is in scripture, how can we think about or desire to bring God's kingdom down to earth?

The enemy will not see you vanish into God's company without an effort to reclaim you.
—C. S. Lewis

The virtual reality of our world is powerful, even though it does not last nor give us fulfillment found in God's kingdom. Although Satan is sometimes among us as a "roaring lion," he more frequently comes as an "angel of light." His deceptively "good" influence has reigned throughout history and in life as we know it today. By his influence we are pulled away from God to thoughts, images and philosophies that eventually lead to emptiness and spiritual death. According to the research of George Barna in his book *What Americans Believe*, "...three out of five adults are inclined to disbelieve in the existence of Satan." Because modern societies tend to discount the authority of scripture and the supernatural, we should not be surprised that many people either do not understand what Satan is like, or discount him entirely. This, of course comes under the guise of more enlightened thinking. The truth is that Satan is a powerful foe of God's, and Jesus has disarmed his power and influence over us through His triumph on the Cross (Colossians 2:14–15). If we want to participate in God's kingdom, we must pray for deliverance from temptation and Satan. God delights to answer this prayer.

Watch and pray so that you will not fall into temptation. The spirit is willing, but the body is weak.
—Matthew 26:41

2. Relate What You've Learned to Your Life

a. *Identify* one useful thing you learned in this lesson.

b. *Name* an area of your life where you would like to see God's kingdom more fully expressed. How can you apply what you've learned to praying for yourself in this situation?

3. Pray for Others

Identify someone you know who is being sorely tested. *Pray* for that person each day this week. *Record* how God speaks to you in the space below. Is there an encouraging step God is asking you to take?

GROUP LEARNING

Form small groups of four. *Read* Cory's story.

> Cory is thirty-three years old. He was reared in a Christian home and he became a Christian as a teenager. He continues to attend church and there are certain social issues he knows the Bible speaks clearly about, but he doesn't want to look at them. He has many non-Christian friends who are aware he is a Christian. They want to know his position on these social concerns, but Cory avoids a dialogue. He thinks he can have a "spiritual" relationship with God without having to look at these issues.

Answer the following questions:

a. What is Cory tempted to "think"?

b. What is Cory tempted to "feel"?

c. What is Cory tempted to "do" as a result?

d. What does it cost Cory to stay like this?

e. What does it cost Cory's non-Christian friends?

f. How would you pray for Cory?

Additional Thoughts

LESSON SIX
Praying in God's Symphony

Read the FOCUS. *Mark* what is useful to you.

FOCUS

> ***There is, of course, much more to prayer than the Lord's Prayer. It is a prayer that teaches us to pray. It is a foundation of the praying life: its introduction and its continuing basis. It is an enduring framework for all praying. You only move beyond it provided you stay within it. It is the necessary bass in the great symphony of prayer. It is a powerful lens through which one constantly sees the world as God himself sees it.***
> **—Dallas Willard**

I was preparing to teach a conference in the coming weekend and was behind in my preparation. My husband and I had tickets for the Los Angeles Philharmonic that evening. Should we go, or should we stay home so I could keep working? We finally made the decision to go; it was a tremendous step of faith for me. At the concert, listening to a Shostakovich symphony my weary and disgruntled spirit took wings. I was literally transported into a completely different attitude and point of view. I touched the arm of the stranger next to me and asked, "Can you even imagine writing something this beautiful and this complex?" "Absolutely not," he replied. I wondered how the orchestra felt as they worked together to play this phenomenal piece of music.

A more important question in light of *Transforming Dialogue,* is "How might you and I feel playing in the symphony of God's kingdom?" It's the most beautiful, most satisfying music we will ever play or hear. To enter into a dialogue with God eventually leads us to see the world as God himself sees it, *and to see our part in bringing His kingdom into it.* We begin the journey with an instrument God places in our hand. At first we don't know what the instrument is. We open the case, without knowing what to do. We try to blow the horn or beat the drum, and even if we get a sound, it isn't very pleasing to us. We take lessons, and we begin to make progress. There are times when the lessons seem tedious, and times when the effort seems too great. We want to quit. We may even bow out for awhile. But, deep inside we know that we *can* make music.

So, we go back to the lessons. We join a band at school and it feels much better to make music with others. Other band members help us keep going as we work together as a team. One day we are invited to join an orchestra. We are amazed at how much progress we're making, alone and together. *One day, we're capable of playing a symphony!* We can't play every part in the orchestra, but we can play our part. After we play concerts, people come up and tell us how inspired they were by the music and how glad they were that they came.

I learned about symphonies by this process. The first time I picked up a flute, I could get no sound. I remember the process as I have just described. It's similar to learning how to pray, where the investment in doing it is far greater. With prayer it's wise to keep eternity in mind.

When we pray for the kingdom of God to come down to this earth in our lives we are making an *eternal* investment. God's kingdom has no beginning and no end. When our human lives come to a close, that phase of kingdom living will end, *but there is eternity ahead of us.* In scripture, we discover that we will reign with God forever. We will participate with him in his ongoing creative plan for the universe. Our role in eternity depends upon what we do now. To the degree that we pray for His kingdom to come into our lives, to the degree that we surrender to His will, we are preparing to live in His kingdom in heaven. The lessons in prayer we learn now require dialogue. Imagine how difficult it would be to learn to play a musical instrument without feedback. We would have no idea how we are progressing or what we need to do next.

We know that messages of radio and television programs are passing through our very bodies and brains at all hours of the day, messages that an appropriate receiver appropriately tuned could pluck from the air we breathe. What an apt picture is this, it seems to me, of the human being in relation to God: showered with messages that simply go right through us or by us. We are not attuned to God's voice. We have not been taught how to hear it.
—Dallas Willard

"If you want to make a sound with the flute, blow into it like you would a coke bottle."

"Here's how to hold the flute so you hands don't get tired.

"Tighten your lips in order to play the higher notes . . ."

In our final lesson on prayer, we will look at what we must do if we are to pray in God's symphony and we will discover guidelines for recognizing how God speaks to us. Regardless of where you are on your spiritual journey, you can play your part in God's symphony. May God give you grace as you pick up your instrument and make music.

QUIET TIME FOR FOCUS

1. Summarize What Was Useful to You in the FOCUS

Summarize what you marked as important to you in the FOCUS.

2. Identifying Our Instruments in God's Symphony

Music is the harmonious voice of creation; an echo of the invisible world; one note of the divine concord which the entire universe is destined one day to sound.
—Mazzini

a. *Imagine* that you are playing in an orchestra that's performing the symphony entitled "I Am A Child In Abba Father's Everlasting Kingdom." What instrument would you like to play?

b. *Name* a familiar song that best describes how you would feel playing with this orchestra. (For example: *To Dream the Impossible Dream, Amazing Grace . . .*)

c. *Examine* what you are willing to do in order to play this symphony.

3. Pray for Guidance with This Lesson

Write a prayer, asking God for what you need Him to teach you about praying in His symphony.

PERSONAL STUDY

1. How Faith Influences Prayer

> ***I prayed for faith, and thought that some day faith would come down and strike me like lightening. But faith did not seem to come. One day I read in the tenth chapter of Romans, "Now faith cometh by hearing, and hearing by the Word of God." I had closed my Bible and prayed for faith. I now opened my Bible, and began to study, and faith has been growing ever since.***
> **—D. L. Moody**

Read the following. *Mark* what strikes you as important.

At the core of the biblical word "faith" is *firmness, reliability, and steadfastness.* In experience, faith is like an anchor that's attached to God, our solid rock (Deuteronomy 32:4, Psalm 18:2, Isaiah 26:4). To have faith in God means that we anchor ourselves to God and take hold of Him with conviction and confidence, even when our boat hits storms and rough seas. We grow in our ability to exercise faith. It's an area of "slow knowledge" and we need to persevere. When we believe God in the middle of a tough spot, we cling to Him in prayer and are transformed by holding on and being *faith*ful. Since the Bible is God's revelation to us of Himself, our ability to have faith rests on having a biblical understanding of God. We exercise faith when we follow the principles of scripture. The only way to grow in faith is to identify our needs and concerns and pray about them. The Lord's Prayer gives us the basic guidelines for how to form our requests. Our faith will grow as we pray along these lines.

a. *Read* Hebrews 11:1–2, 6. *State* what these verses say about faith.

b. *Explain* why faith is important:

<u>To the one praying:</u> <u>To God:</u>

2. The Prayer Life of Jesus

a. *Read* Matthew 14:23, Luke 5:16, 6:12 and 9:28. *Describe* how Jesus prayed.

Read the following paragraph. *Mark* what is useful to you.

Jesus has made more impact on the world than any other religious leader who ever lived. Scripture reveals Jesus as, "Who, being in very nature God, did not consider equality with God something to be grasped, but made himself nothing, taking the very nature of a servant, being made in human likeness" (Philippians 2:6–7). Laying aside His divinity for the time He lived on earth, Jesus had a mission to fulfill. He was to dwell among us and reveal what God is like. He did this through His life, His death, and His resurrection. During His time on earth, He was limited by His humanity. Everything Jesus did then, He did through the power of the Holy Spirit, in which He received in answer to His prayer to His Abba Father.

I have so much to do today that I must set apart more time than usual to pray.
–Martin Luther

b. *Review* your comments in the QUIET TIME FOR FOCUS section. *Identify* what God might be saying to you through the example of Jesus' life of prayer.

3. Instructions Preceding The Lord's Prayer

Read Matthew 6:5–8, in which Jesus gives an introduction to the Lord's prayer. *Answer* the following questions.

a. What guidelines for prayer does Jesus give?

b. What does the word "when" (v. 7) indicate to you?

c. What might you need to change if you decided to follow this instruction?

Man is never so tall as when he kneels before God and never so great as when he humbles himself before God. And the man who kneels to God can stand up to anything.
—Louis H. Evans

d. After your study of the Lord's prayer, what do you think is the benefit of following *this* instruction?

4. Instructions Concluding The Lord's Prayer

Read Luke 11:5–13.

a. *List* some attitudes and emotions that prompted the man to seek bread for his guest.

b. *Use* a dictionary to define the following words. What is Jesus teaching about prayer from verses 9 and 10?

Ask

Seek

Knock

c. *Name* some attitudes and emotions you would need to be that energetic in prayer.

d. *Contrast* the man in the house with God as He is described in verses 11–13. What do you discover?

5. Recognize God's Voice

Read the paragraph below. *Mark* what strikes you as important.

God can use anything to speak to us; however the primary way is through scripture. As we read it, we will learn to know when God is speaking specifically to us. My Bible is filled with underlined verses because God lifted the words off the page and said, "*This is for you today.*" Whenever I sense God speaking to me, I always check to see if it is consistent with scripture. The Bible doesn't speak about every issue we will face in life, but it does tell us what God is like, what His kingdom is like and the character He wants to develop in us so that we can live in His kingdom now. Scripture is meant to be read in its entirety and throughout a lifetime. The more familiar you are with scripture, the more adept you will be in recognizing God's voice.

a. *Read* James 3:17–18 which gives what Myra Boone describes as "a screening device that helps us discern when God is speaking to us." *Describe* the type of dialogue you might expect from God as He is described here.

b. *Name* a situation in your life that needs wisdom. Based on this scripture, *identify* what God might be saying to you now about how to pray regarding it.

FOLLOW THROUGH

Read the following summary. *Mark* what is useful to you.

> ***A human life, filled with the presence and power of God, is one of God's choicest gifts to His church and to the world.***
> **—A.T.Pierson on George Müller's life**

I. SUMMARY

George Müller is one of the most amazing, inspiring examples of what can happen when a person is committed to a life of praying for God's kingdom to come to earth. He was born in Prussia in 1805, and became a Christian twenty years later. The plight of orphans tugged at his heart. Müller prayed about his desire to do something for them.

He eventually built orphanages that housed 2,000 children and supported many Christian workers. He circulated thousands of Bibles and literature and established and maintained schools for poor children. Amazingly, all the money for every building, all the food for every child, and all the supplies for the workers were provided solely in answer to his prayers. He never made a public appeal or collected any money. During his ministry, he raised $7,000,000 through prayer. Listen to what he says about his faith. He insisted that all believers have access to the same faith as his.

> ***I believe the most adequate description of prayer is simply. "Talking to God about what we are doing together."***
> **—Dallas Willard**

"My faith is the same kind of faith that all God's children have had. . . . mine may be more strongly exercised."

Abba Father has given you an instrument to play in the symphony of His kingdom. The people in your life, your interests and your concerns are where you will play your music. Faith in God is like a muscle that develops with use. The food supplying energy to the muscle is scripture where we learn what to pray for. The same God who heard the prayers of Jesus and George Müller is waiting to hear your requests. His greatest delight is to answer!

2. Determine What Was Most Useful to You

a. *Review* the lessons. *Identify* and *prioritize* the three things most useful to you in this study.

   1.
   2.
   3.

b. For the most important priority, *state* one thing you could do every day to put this learning into practice.

3. Get Intentional About Praying

a. How about *setting aside* a specific time and place where you can pray alone and quietly. *Select* a time when you know you will be alert (Your living room at 6 A.M.—or 10 P.M. if you're a "night person", 12:15 in your car in the parking lot during the noon hour…)

b. *Choose* the amount of time you will spend in prayer. (Be reasonable. Choose a time that offers you a realistic opportunity for success. If you are new to prayer, start with five or ten minutes. If you are further along in your prayer journey, select an amount of time that is consistent with your commitment to pray.)

To pray is the greatest thing we can do, and to do it well, there must be calmness, time, and deliberation.
—E. M. Bounds

c. *Purchase* a notebook to use as a prayer journal. (Don't make this complicated— a simple spiral notebook will work.)

d. *Take* your prayer journal to your quiet place for prayer. *Enter* the date. *Name* a person or problem you are truly interested in and would like to do something about. As God begins to speak to you (keep James 3:17–18 and other scriptures in mind), *record* what He says and *date* each entry. You may find it helpful to write your requests in one color of ink, and God's response in another color. As God answers your prayers, *record* the date and the answer.

GROUP LEARNING

Form small groups of four. *Read* the following story.

Bill and Margie own a small business and lately things have been tough. Key suppliers have let them down, two of their best workers quit, and now they're getting complaints from some of their regular customers. Bill and Margie disagree about some important issues in their business and their family, so there's tension between the two of them at home and at work. Margie is exhausted from trying to run their home and work in the business. They both worry that their three children are getting the short end of the stick. They used to attend church occasionally, but haven't gone in a long time. Right now they feel like nothing is going right for them.

a. Based on your study of *Transforming Dialogue*, how are Bill and Margie's needs addressed in the Lord's prayer?

   Our father in heaven
   Hallowed be your name
   Your kingdom come, your will be done
   on earth as it is in heaven
   Give us this day our daily bread
   Forgive us our debts
   As we also have forgiven our debtors
   And lead us not into temptation,
   But deliver us from the evil one

b. *Place* an asterisk(*) by the ones you think might require the persistent prayer Jesus referred to in Luke 11.

c. If you were Bill or Margie, *decide* how you might fit a Matthew 6:6 prayer time ("*But when you pray, go into your room, close the door and pray to your Father, who is unseen. Then your Father, who sees what is done in secret, will reward you.*") into your day.

Additional Thoughts

Appendix

COMING HOME TO ABBA FATHER

My story of coming home to Abba Father is similar to the prodigal son in Luke 15. Raised in the church, under the influence of a godly grandmother, I heard that God loved me. But I was not ready to receive it then. I didn't have a father like the one in Luke 15 (Lesson 2). Both of my parents were alcoholics and I suffered the abuse and neglect of living in that situation. Consequently I didn't feel good about myself, nor "worthy" to come into God's presence.

I compensated by creating my own "virtual reality" and becoming a high achiever and making a life that looked presentable on the outside. Inside I was terribly lonely and unfulfilled. Eventually, I had the same experience as the prodigal son: one day I "came to myself" (Luke 15:17 NRSV) and knew that I had to take my imperfect and bruised self and place it into God's hands. Sin had kept me in a spiritually distant land. But God came near to me through the gospel of Jesus Christ, as He longs to for all of us.

In the Bible, sin means *missing God's mark*. Imagine that your life is like a target. To sin is to miss God's target, God's glorious standard, for *your* life. We commit sins whenever we minimize God and His kingdom. We can do it actively or passively. When we, either through intention or ignorance, live according to our own

desires and rules, we minimize God, fail to hit God's target, and live outside His kingdom. In Lesson 3, we discover how common it is to build our own kingdom apart from God. About the pervasive presence of sin, the Bible says, "For *all* have sinned; *all* fall short of God's glorious standard (Romans 3:23 NLB). SIN alienates us from the loving presence of our Abba Father.

"Come to me now," Jesus says. "Acknowledge and accept who I want to be for you: a Savior of boundless compassion, infinite patience, unbearable forgiveness, and love that keeps no score of wrongs. Quit projecting onto Me your own feelings about yourself. At this moment your life is a bruised reed and I will not crush it, a smoldering wick and I will not quench it. You are in a safe place."
—Brennan Manning

In the gospel of Jesus Christ, God provides the way to return to Him. The apostle Paul declared the gospel ". . . is the power of God for the salvation of everyone who believes" (Romans 1:16). The gospel proclaims the good news that Jesus died for our sins that He was buried, that He was raised on the third day according to the Scriptures, and that He appeared to many witnesses after His resurrection (I Corinthians 15:3–8).

The personal significance of the gospel is that Jesus bore *our* sins when He suffered and died on the cross. At that time, Jesus carried all the sins impacting our lives: the sins committed against us, and the sins we commit against God, others, and ourselves. But that is not all. Jesus not only died, He rose again. He was declared with power to be the Son of God by his resurrection from the dead (Romans 1:4). His empty tomb establishes His place above all other religious leaders in history. When Jesus rose from the dead, He broke the grip of sin and made the resurrection power of God available to us. Through faith in Jesus we can be saved, moment by moment, by His life. We can be forever united with our Abba Father, both in this world and in the one to come.

The salvation of Jesus is a gift. We cannot buy it; we cannot earn it. The Bible makes it clear that in order to possess the gift we must fully *receive* it. The word *receive* means "to possess in the sense of taking ownership." This is what the prodigal son did when he returned home and became an active member of his father's household. This is what we must also do.

"... to all who received him, to those who believed in his name, he gave the right to become children of God ..."
—John 1:12

These three simple words summarize the first necessary steps of receiving God's salvation.

"Sorry"

You must apologize to God for the ways you have broken His law and built your own kingdom instead of His. Your sincere apology will be evident as you turn away from everything that you know displeases Him. The Bible calls this *repentance.*

"Thank you"

You need to acknowledge that Jesus gave up His life for *you. Your* sins were laid on Him on the cross; He died there in *your* place. Through His resurrection, He has made it possible for you to have new life in the Holy Spirit. You need to thank Jesus for His gifts of forgiveness, freedom from sin, and the Holy Spirit.

"Please"

Jesus said, "Here I am! I stand at the door and knock. If anyone hears my voice and opens the door, I will come in and eat with him, and he with me" (Revelation 3:20). Jesus never forces His way into our lives. Instead, He invites us to be His friend. You can receive His invitation by asking Him to please come and live inside your heart by His spirit.

If you are ready to say these three words, here's a simple prayer that will help you receive God's salvation:

Lord Jesus Christ, I am sorry for the ways I have broken Your law. (Take time to ask forgiveness for the specific things that come to your mind.) Please forgive me for my sin. Help me to turn away from what I know to be wrong. Thank You for dying on the cross for me so that I can be forgiven and set free from sin. Please come into my life through the Holy Spirit. Empower me to be a fully functioning person in Your kingdom. Thank you, Lord Jesus. Amen.

When you pray this prayer, God's Spirit will come to dwell inside you. He is the energy of God, given to empower you to live the Christian life. Paul refers to the Holy Spirit in Philippians 4:13 when he says, "I can do everything through Him who gives me strength." The Holy Spirit guides us into God's truth (John 16:13). He is our divine counselor, who always remains with us to give us whatever support we need (John 14:16). He even prays for us according to God's will (Romans 8:26–27).

These are some important things you can do to strengthen your decision to receive Jesus into your life and grow spiritually.

- *Read* your Bible daily. Then, *do* what it says. God will become real to you as you obey Him. Start reading the bible by committing to a regular time. Begin with only five or ten minutes, and build from there.

- *Pray* for your needs. Follow the guidelines for prayer you are learning in this study. Reading the Bible regularly will help you know how to pray.

- *Find* a church and begin *attending* regularly. Ask God to help you discover the best church for you. Respected Christian friends may have valuable suggestions for you.

- *Tell* the important people in your life that you have become a Christian. Own it by sharing it with your loved ones.

- *Persevere* when things get difficult. The Christian life is lived by faith. Some days or periods of our lives are more challenging to our faith than others. Jesus promised that He would never leave or forsake those who have put their faith in Him (Hebrews 13:5). *Seek* God's strength in difficult times. You will discover through perseverance His constant presence.

Life Design Leader's Guide

You are about to begin the rewarding task of leading adults through a Bible study. Even the most rewarding tasks come with a measure of apprehension. If you are anxious about leading this study, be encouraged to know that great leaders in the Bible like Moses, Peter, and Paul felt the same way. Just as God's resources were ample for them, they are also ample for you.

It's also quite natural to be excited about being a small group leader. For many adults, the most effective learning occurs in small groups. These lessons are designed to help people learn the truths of scripture and integrate them into their lives. God has gifted you with skills and abilities to lead a group of adults in their spiritual growth process of maturing in Jesus. Think of your leadership as a gift to them. This *Leader's Guide* provides essential information to equip you to lead them effectively.

Your Personal Preparation to Lead

1. Prayerfully, carefully work through each activity in each section of the lesson. Seek first to understand what God is saying to you in the lesson. Ask Him to show you how to apply the lesson personally. As you do so, you will be able to guide others in the same process.

2. Read through the *Leader's Guide* for each lesson prior to leading it. This will show you how the lesson fits together, and you will get further insight about how to time and lead it effectively. (These notes aren't meant to be read in your small group. However, you may want to refer to them in situations where they are useful.)

3. Mark the Activities in the lesson that have the greatest priority for your group. If time runs short, you will know where to focus your discussion.

4. Pray for each member in your group, using as a guide the insights you received as you studied the lesson. Pray for their growth as they study and participate in the discussions.

5. Build a supportive, personal relationship with members of your group. This will encourage them to attend and participate in the group and help you to understand how best to support their spiritual growth. There are many ways to build relationships: calling people by name, affirming their responses in class, speaking with them personally at each group meeting, phone calls and cards are some natural ways to establish that you appreciate and care for each member of the group.

Leading the Lesson

1. Begin and end the lesson on time. When you are prompt, your group will make an extra effort to be on time. Set the precedent for this in your first meeting and maintain it.

2. Let your group know that diversity in the group and the insights of each member are an asset. Each person can gain from this rich body of experience. Tell the members that you will regularly invite their participation since this is not a lecture class.

3. Ask your group to refrain from negative comments about other churches and religions. Comments like these can alienate others in the group.

4. Encourage several responses to the activities: *"Let's hear more ideas," "Another thought," "A different point of view."*

5. There are small group procedures that will involve maximum sharing in a small group. *Everyone* will share when they are one of a pair discussing familiar information; *almost everyone* will share when they are in a small group of four; *many* find it difficult to share in a group of five or more. These lessons are designed for the maximum participation that's essential for adult learning.

6. Use lavish affirmation whenever possible. It is often difficult for people to feel comfortable expressing their ideas and feelings about the Bible. What might seem lavish to you could be exactly the level of encouragement a participant needs.

7. Don't reject an incorrect or inappropriate answer. Counter it with a question. *"Which verse has led you to this conclusion?" "What do others of you think about this?"* It's also possible to correct an answer that contains some truth by taking a part that is true and turning it around for further discussion in the group. *"Jim sees the challenge contained in this scripture. What do the rest of you think?"*

8. Be encouraging when people resist change. These lessons are designed for personal and spiritual growth. It's natural to face resistance. Accept the feelings that are expressed as part of the growth process. Encourage people in the growth you see and accept their pace. *"Larry, we can see your struggle from what you have shared. Growth isn't easy. We'll be praying with you in this."*

9. Stick with the lesson topic. Each lesson title contains the "great truth" in scripture you will study. Each activity in the lesson will relate to this truth. Your class members will appreciate it when you keep the discussion to the lesson topic. Intervene quickly if someone changes the topic. *"Sarah has introduced another topic here. Perhaps we can discuss this further after we've finished the lesson. Let's return now to activity . . ."*

10. Allow for silence in your discussion. Silence gives us a chance to reflect on what has been said. Important insights require reflection. This kind of pause is quite natural. In a group people can tolerate about 15 seconds of silence before someone will break the tension by speaking. In authentic learning, silence is as necessary as speech. When there is a pause in speaking, welcome it as a sign of people processing what they are learning.

Timing the Lesson

The following schedule is suggested for small groups that meet for 90 minutes:

- 15 minutes: Gathering and refreshments
- 10 minutes: Quiet Time for Focus
- 20 minutes: Personal Study
- 15 minutes: Follow Through
- 15 minutes: Group Learning
- 15 minutes: Group Prayer

If you have a shorter time period, adjust the time accordingly and try to cover each part of the lesson. You can vary the timing according to your schedule. Some variations might be to take two weeks for each lesson or discuss fewer activities in the lesson. Knowledge of the needs of the individuals in your group will help you determine which activities you might eliminate. *It is more important to have good interaction on fewer activities than to rush through just to complete the entire lesson.*

Lesson design

Each of the four segments of the lesson has an important purpose.

- **QUIET TIME FOR FOCUS** enables students to identify where they stand in relationship to the topic to be studied.

- **PERSONAL STUDY** gives students a biblical understanding of the topic and it provides a basis for the rest of the activities in the lesson.

- **FOLLOW THROUGH** provides a guideline for students to integrate into their lives what they have learned.

- **GROUP LEARNING** gives the group an experience to transfer what they have learned into a contemporary context and expand their understanding of the lesson topic through the insight of other group members.

I've also included this additional section on prayer in the *Leader's Guide*.

Pray for Each Other

In the *Leader's Guide*, each lesson will give instructions you can use or adapt to lead your group in praying for each other. The uniqueness of each group will determine when its members are ready to pray together. Some groups are ready to pray together in their first meeting, other groups may not be ready to pray aloud together until they have met a few times. Get to know the people in your group, and respect the process that may be required for them to take the important step of praying together. The *Leader's Guide* will provide prayer exercises to guide you in this sensitive task.

LESSON ONE:

Warm Up for Transforming Dialogue

The tone you set for your first meeting will suggest to your group what they might expect in subsequent weeks. You can demonstrate an attitude of confidence by:

- Having alert posture;
- Maintaining eye contact with each person in the group;
- Speaking in a clear, audible voice;
- Demonstrating a positive and open attitude;
- Calling people by name. Provide name tags and use them each time you meet.

In this introductory lesson we plan to do the following:

- *Discover* our natural approach to learning;
- *Name* which kind of knowledge, "fast" or "slow," we are most comfortable with;
- *Identify* key discussion points from the FOCUS;
- *Name* our expectations for this study;
- *Share* in pairs, groups of four, and the whole group.

This warm up activity is directly related to the study on prayer. It helps us discover how we approach learning. Begin your group by reading this short fable aloud. You might want to read the entire fable yourself or have volunteers read one paragraph. *Form* pairs and have them share which creature they most identify with. Set a time limit, no more than 5 minutes for sharing in pairs and alert them when they are half way through so that each person has an opportunity to share. Then, have them introduce themselves to the whole group and explain their selection. *Respond with lavish affirmation to each person who shares.* Set an encouraging precedent from the beginning of your small group.

PREFACE

Read the instructions in a clear voice and ask if there are any questions. Tell them they will have a few minutes to read the preface silently. When they are finished, *form* small groups of three or four to share their response. Give them about an eight minute time frame for sharing, and let them know when it's mid-point. After eight minutes, give those who want an opportunity to share their insights. *The learning principle here is that adults learn when they are personally engaged in a subject; participation leads to engagement.*

By now, you have used three different kinds of small groups: pairs (activity 1), groups of three or four (activity 2), and sharing in the large group (all participants in Activity 1; some in activity 2). From the beginning you are establishing that this is a group where every person participates.

FOCUS

Read the instruction at the top of the FOCUS and have the group read the FOCUS silently. This reading will take two to three minutes. When finished *form* "new" pairs to share on the activities that follow. Forming new pairs enables group members to interact with everyone and will avoid cliques forming within your small group. Again, set a time limit and give them an opportunity to share with the larger group at the end of this time.

The second section of the FOCUS introduces the topics to be studied in the Lord's Prayer. *Read* the instructions and point out the activity on the following page. At the end of the reading, *ask* the large group what they marked as important. You will likely experience that sharing in the large group is more spontaneous than it might be because people are accustomed to sharing in pairs and small groups of four.

For the last learning activity, read the instructions and give your group a few minutes of silence to review the chapter and write down what they want to learn or accomplish in the study. Ask for those who would like to share this information with the group.

If you are leading a group of people who are not familiar with Life Design study books, you will need to interact with them about *How*

Transforming Dialogue Is Designed. Since it's a preparation for doing the remaining lessons, you will need to call it to the attention of your group by:

- Telling the group that the following lessons will be different because there is personal study preparation to do before coming to the group. Encourage them to take time to work on the lesson throughout the week. The Group Learning section will be done together in the group. Ask them to get started on the lesson right away so they will have the advantage of not rushing through the lesson.
- Turning to *How Transforming Dialogue Is Designed*, and asking them to read it before they do the next lesson.
- Telephoning each member of the class within the next few days and asking if they have any questions about the group or the lesson.

Pray for Each Other (15 minutes)

Praying for each other is vital to the spiritual growth of individuals and your group. This Leader's Guide will contain suggested prayer exercises designed to get each person involved in praying. Use wisdom and courtesy in how you apply the exercise to your group. We want to draw people into deeper fellowship with God, and it requires sensitive leadership to engage the less experienced people in your group in prayer. These prayer exercises build on each other each week, beginning with silent prayer and moving through subsequent weeks until finally the group will be able to pray aloud together. Prayer is a highly individualized but important part of your learning group experience. Approaching it respectfully and purposefully will help maintain your group members' comfort concerning its practice.

Prayer Exercise for Introductory Lesson

Invite your group to form pairs and take one minute for silent prayer for their partner as they begin this study. At the conclusion of that time, pray a one sentence prayer thanking God for how He will answer these prayers in the coming week. Keeping your prayer short will demonstrate a way to pray aloud that will seem attainable to the members of your group, even if they have not had experience praying in a group. Ask your group to pray for the same person during the week. Tell them that in the following weeks, opportunities will be made available in the group for any who wish to pray aloud for each other.

LESSON TWO:
Up Close and Personal

In this lesson, we will learn how to relate to God as "up close and personal" as we:

- *Examine* the Lord's prayer with a relational emphasis;
- *Analyze* what it means to pray to our "hallowed" Father in heaven;
- *Compare* the characteristics of our earthly father with our perception of our heavenly Father;
- *Share* and *pray* for each other in the group.

Please keep these learning objectives in mind as you prepare to lead your group through this lesson.

QUIET TIME FOR FOCUS (10 MINUTES)

1. Summarize What Was Useful to You in the FOCUS

Have your group form pairs to share on this activity. After sharing in pairs, give them an opportunity to share with the whole group. Your affirmation to their responses will give them the confidence to express their ideas, feelings and experiences with the group.

2. Look at Your Experience with God as Your Heavenly Father

The primary purpose of this activity is self-reflection, so you will not need to take a lot of time for this activity to be shared in group. Completing the sentences in this activity may be difficult for people who are new to Bible study or who have not thought about the connection between their human father and God as Father. You will need to be sensitive and positive as you lead this section. This section of each lesson challenges us to explore feelings, personal experiences and opinions in new ways.

Spiritual growth occurs when we see ourselves, God, and our world clearly and take appropriate action. Working through this activity helps us do this. You can introduce the activity like this: *"In this activity we looked at our experience with God as our heavenly Father. What did you learn as you completed the three sentences in this activity?"* Giving them the opportunity to be as general as they like will provide a safe environment for responding. After your introduction, inwardly count slowly to ten. People who want to share their experience need the leader to provide time for them to do so. Silence gives people a chance to collect their thoughts so they can respond thoughtfully. The Follow Through section of the lesson goes deeper into the issues raised here. You could conclude the sharing by saying, *"It's important that we begin our study of an Up Close and Personal relationship with God by looking at our current experience with it."*

3. Pray for Guidance with This Lesson

This particular activity is simply a personal preparation for students before they begin their study. *You may want to offer a brief prayer for your group at this time.*

PERSONAL STUDY (20 MINUTES)

The next two sections deal with integrating what they have studied into their lives. It's important to keep this section lively without appearing rushed. Allow for the time to talk about the activities you carefully choose.

1. The Relational Emphasis of The Lord's Prayer

Activity a. This is an important activity because it deals with the fundamental principle that runs through the entire study. You might ask for a volunteer to read the prayer with an emphasis on the words in *italics*.

Activity b. Since the activity is so important, this is the ideal place to break up into either pairs or small groups of four. Announce how long they have to share in their groups, and make sure you give time at the conclusion for those who want to share with the large group.

2. The Father Heart of God

Although most Christians would say that they believe God is their Father and that His love is unconditional, their *experience* of this is often limited. The activities in this section are "safe" because they deal primarily with what we "think". Move through them as thoroughly as time allows because this information is fundamental to an accurate understanding of our heavenly Father.

3. Pray to Our Father in Heaven

Activities a. and c. provide the content necessary to do the other activities in this section. Allow your discussion to focus on activities c. and d. that apply this information.

It's amazing to consider that God lives in a high and lofty place at the same time He is also present in the atmosphere immediately surrounding us. He is both transcendent and near. When we understand this, it influences how we pray and what we pray for.

4. "Hallowed" Be Your Name

Activity a. Jesus makes the incredible promise, ". . .the Father will give you whatever you ask in my name" (John 15:16). When we *understand* that God's name is "hallowed" it helps us form the kind of prayers God delights to answer. Using God's name in prayer is a difficult concept for us to grasp. Sometimes we tack the phrase, *"I pray this in Jesus name"* onto the end of a prayer without having a clue as to what this means.

Activities b. through e. When people visualize a biblical scene it becomes more relevant and immediate to them. Isaiah sees God as He really is, God speaks and Isaiah responds. God speaks in a vision and Isaiah is undone. Then He speaks through a seraph and Isaiah is encouraged. This is dialogue. If you have your group form "new" pairs for activity d. in this section, you give your group an opportunity to grapple with this. Make sure to give them an opportunity to share with the whole group at the conclusion of their sharing in pairs. If you are running late, you can limit the sharing with the whole group by saying, "We have time for one or two of you to share your discoveries."

FOLLOW THROUGH (15 MINUTES)

It's crucial that you time your lesson so that you have fifteen minutes for this section. *Establish this priority in this lesson.* When your group realizes that you are going to make this section each week, they will be more willing to tackle the challenges of completing the activities in it.

1. Lesson Summary

Form small groups of four to discuss what was useful in the lesson summary, and allow time for individuals to share their information with the whole group. You can see from this summary that it deals more in depth with what it means to trust God as our heavenly Father. Now that they have studied the scripture, they are better able to grasp what this means.

2. Identify How You Perceive Your Earthly Father and Your Heavenly Father

Since this is a personal activity, it wouldn't be appropriate to call on people to respond to these activities. You will provide a "safe" environment for sharing on this activity if you first ask what was their experience in marking the continuum. After you ask this, briefly share your experience and keep your sharing non-threatening. "I discovered some gaps." "I discovered some similarities." "I discovered how much I don't yet know about God." "I found this challenging."

Then ask who would like to share their discoveries. Again, give an example: "I discovered that my father holds grudges and that makes it hard for me to believe God wants to forgive me." "My father was fair which helps me to believe that God will be fair with me." Affirming everyone who shares is an important reinforcement here.

GROUP LEARNING (15 MINUTES)

This activity provides a safe and easy way to apply what is learned from the study. The case studies in this book are designed to be "close enough to be relevant, and far enough away to be safe." As you break up into small groups of four, people can tackle the problem presented in the case study and learn a great deal from their interaction with each other. Set a time limit for the activity and provide enough time at the end for individuals who want to share to do so.

PRAY FOR EACH OTHER (15 MINUTES)

You will notice that this is an extremely simple exercise. Even the shyest or least experienced person in group prayer will feel comfortable engaging in this prayer exercise.

Form small groups of four. Sit quietly with your eyes closed. Start the time with, "Let's take a few moments of silence to identify with one word the characteristic of God we would like to have." Wait a few moments, and if no one has stated a word, you can get the process moving by stating yours. At the conclusion of this time, you might offer a brief prayer thanking God for being our heavenly Father. (When you keep your prayer brief, you give everybody in the group a model for praying in a group that is attainable.)

The time to share should take five to seven minutes, and the prayer time two minutes at the very most. You should have a few moments left to ask your group who would like to share about their experience with this kind of prayer.

LESSON THREE

Praying with the Biggest Dog

In this lesson we will learn about praying with the "biggest dog" as we:

- *Examine* what living in God's kingdom is like;
- *Determine* the scope of our personal kingdom;
- *Specify* what is involved in praying "Your kingdom come, your will be done on earth as it is in heaven" into our life;
- *Analyze* why there is a conflict between God's Kingdom and ours;
- *Share* and *pray* together in our group.

Please keep these learning objectives in mind as you prepare to lead your group through this lesson.

QUIET TIME FOR FOCUS (10 MINUTES)

1. Summarize What Was Useful to You in the FOCUS

The sharing on this activity need not take long. Form pairs and tell them they have a couple of minutes for sharing. Allow for time at the end for those who want to share with the whole group.

2. Prepare for the Study of God's Kingdom

Sincerely praying for God's kingdom to come and His will to be done in our lives is the most difficult of all prayer requests. We can give lip service to it long before we can say it with a pure heart. This activity helps us take a look at our desire to be independent and self-sufficient. As we will discover in doing the lesson, our need for self-sufficiency is part of what it means to be created in God's image and likeness. This lesson is about harnessing that desire and placing it within the boundaries of God's kingdom.

You will not have time to cover all these questions. However, you can reinforce their value by reminding them that these preparatory questions help us know where we stand in relationship to the topic. When we go into our personal study with this preparation, we are able to look at the Bible with more clarity and focus. It's natural to see a discrepancy in our lives and what the Bible teaches. Seeing the difference is the first important step of spiritual growth.

PERSONAL STUDY (20 MINUTES)

1. Introduction to God's Kingdom

Activity a. Psalm 145 contains a glorious and diverse description of God's kingdom. Seek to pull out the richness of this description because it's the basis for all the work in the lesson. This is the kingdom God calls us to partner with Him in bringing to this earth! What you want to avoid here is one person giving a "list." To get everyone to participate, you could read the exercise and have them identify *one* or *two* characteristics that were appealing or compelling to them. Then ask for each of them to quickly share what they marked. This should take you no more than two minutes.

Activity b. This exercise is important because it reveals that all the potential of experiencing God's kingdom as it's described in Ps. 145 is possible for believers. God wants every believer to comprehend and enjoy who He is and the Kingdom He has made available to us now.

Activity c. This exercise begins to prepare people for the FOLLOW THROUGH section of the lesson.

2. Our Need to Build a Kingdom

Activity a. This activity puts the emphasis on exercising authority over what is in the effective range of our will. When we learn that the only thing we can really control is within our own skin, we can focus on the only thing we can really do something about: how we live our lives before God. We have authority over this. God has given it to us. If we live in God's kingdom we must learn to "subdue" our own lives. It won't take your group long to share on activity a., especially if you ask them to form pairs to do it.

Activity b. This activity can be handled very quickly. How thrilling to know that God put it into our hearts to have a voice, a say over our own lives! No wonder totalitarian governments don't work. It should come as no surprise that we are bent out of shape when someone removes from us the God-given right to have a voice.

3. God's Desires Concerning His Kingdom and Ours

Activity a. This simply brings your group on the same page about the prayer request in this section of the Lord's prayer.

Activity b. Presents a challenge similar to the many we face every day: How do we juggle living in God's will with modern problems? You might have them form quick pairs of four and give them two minutes to work on this. Allow time for people to share with the whole group.

There's a principle in adult education that's important to keep in mind here. *The shorter the time, the higher the energy level in working together.* Since they have all thought about this before hand, they are ready to work quickly now. Too much time given to a learning activity will result in a boring experience, something you want to avoid like the plague!

4. Bring God's Will Down to Earth

These are important and varied characteristics. Again, you want to avoid one person giving a "list." You can move the sharing along by asking for those who would like to call out one attitude or behavior.

5. The Conflict Between God's Will and Ours

These activities deal with how it is possible to overcome our inner tendency to want to live independently from God. Allow as much time as you can for this section.

Activity a. Form either pairs or small groups of four to share what was useful in this section. Do allow time for feedback with the whole group.

Depending on your time you might want to remain in smaller groups for activity b.

Activity b. The first two questions can be answered quickly, but the remaining three will require more time for sharing because they deal with increasingly deeper and more personal levels of learning. Give small groups the opportunity to share with the whole group.

FOLLOW THROUGH (15 MINUTES)

Activity a. Break up into small groups of four to share insights on this section, giving people a chance to share with the whole group. This ensures that your whole group stays cohesive, even when you break up into smaller groups.

Activities b-d. These activities are highly personal. It might be appropriate to remain in smaller groups for sharing on them. Introduce them in a general way because it will give them freedom to share what they are comfortable sharing. If you break up into smaller groups for sharing, allow time at the end for those who would like to share with the larger group.

GROUP LEARNING (15 MINUTES)

Here you get to grapple with a case study that presents an ongoing difficult situation. In all likelihood, Betty isn't going to change very much. She's had 70 or 80 years of strong-willed habits.

Activity a. This exercise presents the opportunity to evaluate how God might be speaking to Carrie. Here are some possibilities: the circumstances Carrie has to live with; her feelings of dissatisfaction about taking the path of least resistance; her fear about praying for God's will and the need to change. Each of these provides Carrie with a need to pray about and an opportunity to *listen* to what God will say in response to her prayer. This activity ties directly into the dialogue dimension of prayer.

Activity b. Here you have the opportunity to analyze "What is Carrie responsible to rule over and subdue?" When we can effectively identify these areas for Carrie, we will be more adept in transferring that information over to our own lives.

Activity c. This activity helps us determine how we might face the fears involved in living under the authority of God's kingdom.

Activity d. Here you will be able to get very specific about how to pray about difficult, ongoing situations. It's when we become specific about our needs in these kinds of situations that we learn to *listen* to what God says in response. The more specific we are in prayer, the better able we are to discern just how God might be speaking.

PRAY FOR EACH OTHER (15 MINUTES)

This prayer exercise is similar to the one given in the last lesson. The principle involved here is safety. If you want each member to participate in the prayer time, you need to provide a safe environment for those who are new to this experience. The fascinating principle about learning that needs to be considered here is that *safety does not mean lack of challenge.* To learn something new there must be a challenge or we get bored and lose interest. So the challenge is helping shy and inexperienced people to feel comfortable and pray in a group, while at the same time helping experienced prayers accept the pace of the *group*. Personal conversations with group members will be most helpful in dealing with these challenges.

First, *form* pairs. *Share* your experience with praying and listening to God during the last week. Allow time for people to share with the whole group.

Form small groups of four. *Sit* quietly with your eyes open this time. After some silence, *speak* a word or short phrase tells what you need from God as you pray for His kingdom to come and His will to be done in your life.

At the conclusion of this time, allow time for feedback in the group. What was their experience of praying with their eyes open? How did they feel limiting themselves to a word or phrase?

LESSON FOUR

The Problem of a Picnic in Pompeii

In this lesson we will learn what the problem with a "picnic in Pompeii" is as we:

- *Examine* the relational dimension of praying for the daily needs of others;
- *Identify* what we need daily to be a fully functioning person in God's kingdom;
- *Analyze* what it means to pray for our forgiveness and why we should forgive those who have sinned against us;
- *Create* a plan, based on our daily needs, for functioning fully in God's kingdom;
- *Share* and *pray* together in our group.

Please keep these learning objectives in mind as you prepare to lead your group through this lesson.

QUIET TIME FOR FOCUS (10 MINUTES)

Now that you have led three lessons, you have a general idea of the purpose of each section and how to time and lead each one. Refer to the notes on QUIET TIME FOR FOCUS on lessons two and three to review how to lead this section. For example, to ensure engagement, form pairs on activity 1 to share the summary, and allow time for anyone who wants to share in the large group.

The emphasis of this lesson is that Jesus teaches us to pray for our daily needs and the needs of others. Our needs in an affluent society are far beyond physical. So, help your group to identify the needs in activity 2.b. Since these are not their personal needs, you can feel free to ask people to call out several in a word or phrase for each of the elements of activity b.

PERSONAL STUDY (20 MINUTES)

1. Pray for What We Need

We have begun this lesson with the doctrine of praying for our daily needs and progressed through the needs of others. You know the needs of the individuals in your group, so this can help you plan your time for activities a. through c. Activity d. provides a good opportunity to form small groups of four.

2. Our Greatest Daily Need

As it turns out, our greatest need every day is to seek God's kingdom and His righteousness. This is a spiritual need. Activity d. helps people look at the emotional aspects of seeking God's kingdom. When we put our name in the text, it heightens our sense of personal responsibility.

3. Our Daily Need for Forgiveness

Our need to pray daily for forgiveness is also a spiritual need. Sin hampers our fellowship with God, and since none of us is perfect, we have a continual need to pray for forgiveness. If you have a beginner's group, this may be new to some in your group. It's true that when we receive Jesus, He cleanses us from all sin. It's also true that we sin every day and need to experience God's cleansing.

4. Common Sins

Activity a. This is an interesting exercise, designed to help people become aware of common sins we all commit.

Activity b. Look for varied answers here. Think of how damaging these sins are on the people who commit them and how painful they are on those whom we inflict them. If you are pressed for time, you might consider just discussing activities a. and d. in this section.

5. Jesus Teaches About Forgiveness

These activities really demonstrate what Jesus meant when He taught us to pray, "as we also have forgiven our debtors." Take as much time as you can with this section, and carefully choose the activities that best fit the needs of your group.

FOLLOW THROUGH (15 MINUTES)

Check the instructions for how to lead this section in Lessons 2 and 3. With activity 2, after you have asked for their "experience" with this activity, you might break up into small groups of four. Ask, "Those of you who feel comfortable, share one or two of the needs you are facing in the next 24 hours."

GROUP LEARNING (15 MINUTES)

The lesson has been directed toward helping us become aware of our needs, the needs of others and praying about them. The scenarios presented here are typical things many of us deal with and we are reminded in them that everything we are faced with holds God's invitation to pray. Every day, we have needs associated with living on a tight schedule, facing poverty and famine in the media, and getting along with people who we feel are insensitive. If you like, you can assign or have each group choose the scenario they want to work on. It would be interesting to have more than one scenario for the whole group to work on. Have the small groups report their work to the whole group. Look to see if they are including the "relational dimension" in their work.

PRAY FOR EACH OTHER (15 MINUTES)

Do you think your group might be ready to pray conversationally? Using dialogue is one of the most enjoyable ways people can pray together. Form groups of four within your small group. The main principles of conversational prayer are:

a. Focus on one person at a time. One person gives a short sentence about a need they want God's help with.

b. Someone else in the group then adds a thought to that request. Then someone adds to that. All the prayers are short.

c. When the praying for that person is complete, someone else brings up a need and the process continues until each person in the group is prayed for.

Here's a sample dialogue to read that will help your group understand what conversational prayer is. Read it to your group before praying.

Sandi: *Lord, when I'm circling around in the parking lot, help me to remember I'm not the only person in the universe.*

Jim: *God, give Sandi the sense of your presence and your love for all people while she moves through her busy schedule.*

Larry: *I feel so much like Sandi, and I just add my prayer that from this moment on she will see parking lots holding your invitation to be patient.*

You have 15 minutes for this section. If you take a couple of minutes to give instructions and ten minutes to pray, you will have a few minutes for feedback.

LESSON FIVE

The Truth Behind Virtual Reality

As we approach the last lessons, encourage your group that the next lesson brings all that they have learned about prayer into focus. Plan a special celebration for your group for your last meeting together.

In this lesson we will learn how to pray about temptation and evil as we:

- *Relate* "And lead us not into temptation, but deliver us from the evil one" to our personal experience;
- *Analyze* God's purpose in testing His people;
- *Examine* Satan's two strategies for evil and *determine* which strategy is most effective with us;
- *Share* and *pray* for ourselves and others regarding the temptations and evil influences in our lives.

Please keep these learning objectives in mind as you prepare to lead your group through this lesson.

QUIET TIME FOR FOCUS (10 MINUTES)

We are moving into deep water with this lesson as we confront the reality of our temptations and Satan. You will need to cover your group in prayer as they do this lesson. I included the gas station story because I wanted to present a model of temptation that would stretch us to see a larger scope of temptations than the ones we all know and are familiar with. Forming pairs for activity 1, will give people the time and conversation they need to engage in group discussion and process where we are going in the lesson.

PERSONAL STUDY (20 MINUTES)

Thoughtfully consider how you will lead your group through this lesson determining which activities are most important and which ones you can eliminate.

1. Pray to Overcome Temptation

Activity 1.b. lends itself well to breaking up in smaller groups. Again, I have included temptations that broaden our understanding.

2. God's Purpose in Testing Us

Activity 2.a. presents God's reasons for testing us, and 2.b. takes us deeper into how testing presents an invitation for growth. If we trust "Abba Father," testing draws us nearer to Him, always within the boundaries of God's love and His holiness.

3. Pray About Evil

This provides the biblical content for activities 4 and 5.

4. How Evil Works in Our World

These scriptures can be gone over quickly; they simply present the ways Satan tries to keep us from living fully in God's kingdom.

5. The Dual Nature of Satan

This is an extremely important activity, so make sure you make time to cover it fully. Activity c. lends itself to smaller group participation.

FOLLOW THROUGH (15 MINUTES)

1. Summary

Form pairs to discuss what was important to you in the summary.

2. Relate What You've Learned to Your Life

Break into groups of four and share how you can apply what you have learned in this lesson to your own life. Encourage your group to share how God is speaking to them this week.

GROUP LEARNING (15 MINUTES)

Cory represents many Christians in the church today. Notice how the activities break down the various ways Cory is tempted. Again, we are expanding our understanding of the scope of temptation.

PRAY FOR EACH OTHER (15 MINUTES)

Use the guide for the last lesson for conversational prayer, but change the emphasis to praying for the area where they are experiencing temptation. Keep the prayer focused on what they are learning. Remind them to pray in one sentence or a phrase. Remember that your goal here is engagement. When I prayed for the woman in the gas station, I prayed with my eyes open so I could discern how to pray. Encourage them to pray for each other with their eyes open. After praying, have them share on how that impacted their prayer.

LESSON SIX

Praying in God's Symphony

In this lesson we will learn how to pray in God's symphony as we:

- *Examine* how the model of Jesus and His guidelines for prayer can influence our practice of prayer;
- *Relate* a biblical "screening device" for discerning God's voice to a prayer situation in our lives;
- *Create* a plan for how to have a daily time of prayer;
- *Evaluate* how our prayers have been impacted by applying the principles in *Transforming Dialogue* to ourselves;
- *Share* and *pray* with each other about issues this lesson raises for us.

Please keep these learning objectives in mind as you prepare to lead your group through this lesson.

QUIET TIME FOR FOCUS (10 MINUTES)

Follow the instructions in Lessons 2 and 3 for how to lead this section. Notice that activity 2 has a playful element. You're celebrating the end of your learning experience.

PERSONAL STUDY (20 MINUTES)

1. How Faith Influences Prayer

The emphasis here is on faith having a biblical base and growing as we pray and exercise it. We have the size of faith we "want" to have. How willing are we to persevere in praying for the things that are important to us?

2. The Prayer Life of Jesus

The purpose of this section is for you to discover that Jesus needed to pray, and that He prayed regularly. He sets the example of regular prayer for us to follow. These activities set us up for the ones that follow.

3. Instructions Preceding The Lord's Prayer

Here we discover that we are to pray regularly in a room by ourselves. This goes against the grain of how most people "want" to pray today. Try to give each activity in this section time for discussion. If time allows, activities c. and d. would work well in small groups of four.

4. Instructions Concluding The Lord's Prayer

Here we discover that we're to pray about the things that move our hearts. We are to listen to what bothers us and pray about it. We are to go deeper and deeper with our requests, giving prayer a priority in our lives. Spend time on activity d. as it points out the difference between "Abba Father" and the man who finally gave his friend some food. Verses 11–13 reveal that God's greatest answer to prayer is giving us a greater experience of His presence as we persevere in prayer.

5. Recognize God's Voice

This is an extremely important activity because it provides a "screening device" for determining the kinds of messages God gives us. In light of your time, you might concentrate on activities a. and b as there's ample personal application to discuss in the FOLLOW THROUGH section.

FOLLOW THROUGH (15 MINUTES)

1. Summary

George Müller's story pulls together all the principles in this lesson. *Form* pairs to discuss this summary.

2. Determine What Was Most Useful to You

These activities help us evaluate what we have experienced in the study. Activity 2.a provides a non-threatening way to engage in an overview of the study. You might ask each person to name one useful thing they learned in the course of this whole study.

3. Get Intentional About Praying

For this activity, you might ask your group what their experience was with these activities which provide a plan for developing a regular time of prayer.

GROUP LEARNING (15 MINUTES)

Activity a. provides the opportunity to review together what we learned in this study. Here are some creative ways Bill and Margie might apply the Lord's Prayer to their situation.

Hallowed be your name—Dissatisfied customers and workers quitting might mean that Bill and Margie are partially to blame. *"Lord, what are we doing that doesn't meet your holy standard? What are we failing to do that falls short of being a Christian and being an example of your name in this situation?"*

Give us this day our daily bread—Bill and Margie need to be praying for each other because they both carry heavy loads. Several "daily needs" are mentioned in this case study.

Forgive us our debts—Bill and Margie are at odds with each other and they have neglected their spiritual needs, so both need to ask for forgiveness for themselves. Both need to forgive each other, and others involved in their situation.

Activity b. will likely reveal that most of the prayers are single or even intermittent requests. This will emphasize the need for us to persevere in praying daily.

Activity c. will help us figure out just how Bill or Margie can actually create a plan to pray every day. If we can do this for them, we can do it for ourselves!

PRAY FOR EACH OTHER (15 MINUTES)

Here's an opportunity to get your group involved in praying in pairs. If you feel members of your group would not be intimidated, ask them to form pairs for conversational prayer. If there are those who haven't yet prayed in the group, encourage them to either form a pair with a close friend in the group or with someone who wants to pray silently. Encourage them to pray in a way most comfortable for them – standing, sitting, eyes open or closed. Ask them to pray about the one thing that most concerns them today.

Bibliography

Boone, Myra, 1999. *Touching the Hem of His Garment—A Guide for Encountering God.* This twelve-week workbook shows how to recognize and listen to God's voice. The book is available through Church Resource Ministries, 1240 N. Lakeview Ave. #120, Anaheim CA 92807-1821.

Cymbala, Jim. *Fresh Wind, Fresh Fire*, 1999. This is an inspiring book about how the Brooklyn Tabernacle uses prayer as the backdrop for their amazing ministry. The true stories in this book will motivate you to pray with effectiveness. It also provides a record of the phenomenal things God is doing right now through the prayers of ordinary people committed to prayer.

Foster, Richard J., 1992. *Prayer—Finding the Heart's True Home.* An outstanding basic book on prayer which covers many kinds of prayers, from the most basic to the deepest. It's a valuable book to have in your library.

Manning, Brennan. *Abba's Child—The Cry of the Heart for Belonging*, 1994. In this heartwarming book, Manning gives us insight about what it means to be a child of Abba Father. If you have ever grappled with your inadequacies and God's claim to love you, you will appreciate this book.

Rice, John R., 1942. *Prayer—Asking and Receiving.* This book may not be in print. It's a basic primer on the practical aspects of prayer and contains wonderful stories of answered prayer.

Thielicke, Helmut, 1953. *The Prayer that Spans the World—Sermons on the Lord's Prayer.* This theological book on the Lord's prayer was written by a German pastor after World War II. It gives marvelous insight into the biblical content of the Lord's prayer, and it also deals with the issues of God's truth versus "virtual reality."

Thompson, Marjorie J. *Soul Feast* 1995. *Soul Feast—An Invitation to the Christian Spiritual Life.* Deals with the basic disciplines of the spiritual life and is written from a feminine perspective. Men and women alike will benefit from reading it.

Willard, Dallas. *In Search of Guidance, 1997.* This is the most outstanding book on the dialogue dimension of prayer I have ever read. Dallas Willard is one of the most substantial voices on Christian spirituality writing today. This is not an "easy" book to read, but if you can stay with it you will find profound wisdom on discovering how God speaks to us.

Willard, Dallas. *The Divine Conspiracy—Rediscovering Our Hidden Life in God,* 1998. This is an incredible book about the kingdom of God. It is not a "quick read" because there is a surprise on every page to mull over. It ranks at the top of the most significant Christian books I've ever read. The meaning of the Lord's Prayer about how to function in the kingdom of God is fully explored.